MW01705006

Treasure Chest

Lloyd Dennis

Treasure Chest of Muskoka Memories

Fox Meadow Creations / Brad Hammond

Published by Brad Hammond and Fox Meadow Creations

Distributed by Fox Meadow Creations
P.O. Box 5401, Huntsville, Ontario P1H 2K7
www.foxmeadowbooks.com / Tel. 705-788-0469

National Library of Canada Cataloguing in Publication Data

Dennis, Lloyd A.
Treasure chest of Muskoka memories / Lloyd Dennis.

ISBN 0-9681452-9-9

1. Dennis, Lloyd A. — Childhood and youth. 2. Muskoka (Ont. : District municipality) — Biography. I. Title.

FC3095.M88Z49 2003 971.3'1603'092 C2003-906785-8

Design and typesetting by Fox Meadow Creations
Front cover photograph © 2003 by Lloyd Dennis, taken by John Carpino
Printed and bound in Canada by Métrolitho

Text typeface is Tyrnavia
Printed on acid-free paper

Printed in Canada

Front Cover

Lloyd's "Treasure Chest" with the mementos of childhood and young adulthood that help him keep alive the memories of those early days.

Title Page

Lloyd's class at the Ullswater school in 1932. Lloyd (marked "x") is in the middle row, centre.

The Dennis family, 1943—Lloyd, in uniform, standing with his brother, Vernon, and his parents near their temporary wartime home on the road to Nobel.

Contents

Lloyd's parents, Alf and Bessie Dennis, and grandparents Louis and Rebecca Grimes in Alf Dennis's first car. Alf sits proudly at the wheel.

Lloyd's parents, Alfred Dennis and Elizabeth Grimes, on the occasion of their wedding, October 14, 1914.

Acknowledgements

They are no longer here; but I am certain that my parents and my brother are with me in spirit as I sprinkle this dust of memory for all to see. They were part of its creation, and I have them to thank for the adventures that were the warp and woof of my life in Muskoka. I must thank also old friends who shared those days with me. Among them are Norma Carrick (Creasor) and Edith Smith (Olsen), who still join me upon occasion to reach back to earlier times.

I also wish to thank the editor of the *Orillia Packet and Times*, Mark Bissett, for permission to use articles that have appeared under my name in recent months. The reception to those encouraged me to place this treasure before you, the reader. Material drawn from other published works of mine is also gratefully acknowledged.

I am also indebted to my daughter Gale Dennis-Thompson for her editorial skill, to my wife, Marilyn, and daughter Susan for their encouragement, and to my indefatigable secretary, Janette Wyville, for the endless trials which my writing presented. Yes, I am still left-handed, and submit my manuscript in longhand.

Lloyd Dennis

Lloyd Dennis with his older brother, Vernon, about 1933.

The Treasure Chest

They came when I was young, this curious crowd. Pushing and shoving, they entered my eager mind and began their long conversion into the golden dust of my memory. Some of them were important agents in the development of my fate, while others were mere wisps of the moment, barely deserving of attention at the time. But, large or small, horrendous or glorious, they crowded in, took their place, and waited.

They were, indeed, a motley mixture. I was born in the bush, and not many years after, during the Great Depression, life for my parents became an endless struggle to survive. Circumstances forced frequent change upon us, so that I was almost guaranteed my full share of memorable events by the time I reached adulthood.

And now this golden dust fills a treasure box of memory. In fact, it has already spilled into a memoir called *Marching Orders*, and dust more recent filled a book called *The Learning Circle*. But these stories couldn't begin to contain all of the bits and pieces of my past. So here I am again, reaching into the treasure chest in search of more dust to sprinkle. Should it fall upon you, I hope that it tickles your fancy.

The Dance

On one star-filled night in 1930, we bundled into the cutter and struck out for the Hall, which lay in the Village of Aspdin, about four miles away. It was really a parish hall, and stood one step down from the Anglican Church that dominated the hill. But it served the community of Aspdin for a variety of purposes, and since it was the only social facility of the area, its regular use elevated it to a more ecumenical title. It was known as "the Hall" to people for miles around. It boasted a driveshed to shelter the horses of its patrons, a woodshed, and an outdoor toilet, or backhouse, for each sex. Small in comparison with more urban facilities, the Hall was the largest community building in the area. Tonight it offered a special treat, which drew the local people like moths to light. It was the Thompson wedding dance.

A night ride in the cutter was a commonplace event at that time. Nevertheless, the experience left imprints on our minds that would remain long after Jessie was dead and gone. It wasn't just the ride. It was the ingredients of the ride that gave it a memorable quality. Taken separately, they were of no great moment; but blended together they attacked the senses of a young boy like the sirens of Odysseus, urging him to ride in the cutter forever.

The most immediate was the sense of warmth provided by the wooden heaters and the covering robe. Huddled like a cocoon on the cutter's floor, and warm in the midst of a frigid night, I could peek out into the darkness and see the stars in the dark sky, like fireflies swimming in a sea of ink. I would cast a wary eye upon the snow-capped stumps and trees that lined the bush road, which Vernon said were really snow ghosts waiting to capture us. His dire description was given credibility whenever Jessie would snort and shy from something that startled her in the night. At such times, I would snuggle down under the rug and doze off, listening to the jingle-jingle-jingle of Jessie's bells, the thud of snow clots thrown against the dashboard by her hooves, and the squeak of the cutter as its runners rubbed the snow. Smell added to the euphoria of the ride. From the robe came the dank odour of horse, sweat and hay, while the hint of scorched paper came from the warm blocks of wood. And when Jessie broke wind, her dual contribution of sound and smell added a pungent presence to the atmosphere that only a horse could offer.

The combination of the ride's ingredients were enough to lull us into a state of blissful somnolence that was finally broken by our father. "Whoa there, Jess!" And as he threw the buffalo robe over the horse in the driveshed, Mother led my brother and me into the place of magic, carrying her basket of contributions to the after-dance lunch, and all the while bombarding us with admonitions about our behaviour and hinting at the consequences should we fail to heed her.

Inside, I was struck by the size of the room, the largest I had ever been in. Lit by a row of kerosene lanterns, and heated by an immense box-stove at the rear, its hardwood floor was sprinkled with a light dusting of dance wax, and its rafters were hung with pink and white streamers that twisted and crossed from wall to wall. People sat along the walls or stood in clusters, exchanging gossip and eyeing newcomers as they entered. I watched as two children turned the floor into a slide, only to have their fun cut short by a box on the ears and a tug into oblivion by a watchful mother. The hall had a stage and it was here that the orchestra had begun to assemble. Already the girl at the piano was sounding "A" for the fiddles of her father and brother, while an uncle picked tentatively on a banjo. Periodically one would squeak out a few bars of jig music, only to stop and adjust his instrument, readying it for the long playing to come.

"Look, Alf," said Mother as she placed her refreshment basket on the stage. "There's the Thompson couple, over there talkin' to the Clarkes. My, she's a pretty young thing. I do hope she hasn't made a mistake with the Thompson boy. Here boys, put this basket back there on the stage with the others. Then you can go and sit with Ken. See, he's over there, behavin' himself, just like you're goin' to. Alf, straighten your tie. We'll go over and pay our respects to the bride and groom."

It was a square dance, and began with a quartet heralding the first set with the opening bars of "Turkey in the Straw." Couples gradually formed squares, urged on by the caller, who constantly begged for "one more couple," or "two more couples" until the floor was full. Suddenly the company of couples so recently rooted in the work of farm and bush, was transformed to a whirling stamping kaleidoscope of colour and rhythm as they responded to the music and its caller. Our parents were in the middle of it, and I had no trouble behaving as I sat transfixed by the spectacle before me. Mother and Dad, so solemn under the ordinary circumstances of life, were actually having fun! There was Dad, coat off and white shirt gleaming, swinging my mom with a happy abandon that seemed almost improper. And Mom, in her new print dress made from material bought in Brown's Store, was laughing. With a feeling of pleasure oddly mixed with embarrassment, I was not sure whether to watch or look away. I decided to watch.

As the evening wore on, we younger children found ourselves laid on the stage like little logs, to sleep our way toward refreshment time. Hot coffee, tea, sandwiches, cookies and cake heralded the end to the dance, and by the time I had drowsed through a sandwich it was time to go. The community poured through the door amid calls of farewell and banter, to be transferred by sleigh and cutter back to a more arduous world. With a "Giddap, Jess," we headed for home.

The magic of the night was almost over. But the sparkling dust of its memory still lingers in my mind.

Off the Record

Just up the road from our house in Martin's Siding lay the Davis farm. It was one of the "established" properties of the village, and it had all the accoutrements of comfort that were bound to impress a young boy in the early thirties.

One of these attractions was a Thomas Edison phonograph. With its curved and varnished cover, it sat grandly on the small table near the window, virtually begging young hands to remove its hood and bare its mystery for all the world to see. Of course, I never yielded to this temptation. Our family visits were much too polite and courteous to permit such liberties. I did, however, yearn for its divine exposure, and fervently hoped that the time would come when Mr. Davis would say, "Would you like to listen to the phonograph?"

Finally, one evening visit paid off with just this invitation, and I sat enthralled as Mr. Davis lifted the wooden cover and exposed Thomas Edison's invention.

It was a simple affair, really, with a horizontal cylinder of shining steel suspended over the machine's deck. Above the cylinder a cap sat poised, to which the master of ceremonies attached a horn. He took what appeared to be a blue grooved tube from its case and slid it onto the cylinder. "Now watch this," he proudly ordered. "There's a needle under that cap, I'm going to lower it down to rest on the tube, crank her up, and let the brake off. Are you all set?"

I was as set as I could be.

Then suddenly, plaintively, and out of thin air, I heard, ever so faintly, the sad lament of "My Bonnie Lies Over the Ocean." Before I had time to recover, I was carried off on a long long trail that was winding to the land of my dreams!

The magic went on, from one song to the next; and just as I was getting used to this moment of magic, my mother said that it was time to go. Slowly I came down to earth as Mr. Davis removed the horn and replaced the cover. The magical machine returned to its customary role as a piece of furniture, and we went home.

When Grandma came to live with us, she brought her horse Jessie, a buggy and a cutter. But she brought something else too; and though I loved Jessie to pieces, this other possession could take me where no horse could go. It was a gramophone, a descendant of Mr. Edison's phonograph. It looked quite grand, standing there in the corner overpowering the rest of the modest furniture, with its graceful carved legs and tapered top. It sported a grilled screen of wooden filigree above two cabinet doors; and to the uninitiated, it was just that—a cabinet with two nice doors. Inside that screen was a covered opening that grew even narrower till it disappeared upwards toward the back of the cabinet.

But the treasure lay on the shelves behind the doors. There I found the magic of music that is in my mind still. Round, flat records, each in its green paper case, were stacked on the two shelves, just itching to be released and spun by a curious boy. Their freedom was at hand. Then I became *their* captive.

Oh, it didn't happen immediately. Grandma had a loving but forbidding presence about her, and playing the gramophone was akin to a visit to town. It was an event to be won, then savoured. But finally Grandma moved to Aunt Flossie's, leaving the treasured instrument behind. With a new sense of adventure, I got to open the top where a green turntable awaited the first record. An arm reached out with a contraption that held a needle set and ready to go to work. Lying beside the turntable was a small crank. "I'll just take that crank out and screw it in place on the side of the cabinet," said Dad. "Then we'll wind her up and play 'Turkey in the Straw.' Mother and I danced to that tune at the Thompson wedding dance, remember?"

I remembered. In fact, it was indelibly etched upon my mind as were a number of other tunes that I found among Grandma's records. "When the Work's All Done This Fall," "Red River Valley" and "There's A Long Long Trail A Winding" vied with others to lock themselves in my memory forever. On cold winter days or long, lamp-lit evenings, my parents would let me indulge my love for those precious records, till they must have secretly prayed that Grandma would come and reclaim her property. But in those days of Depression, I suspect that even those paltry tunes from the old gramophone were better than no sound at all.

As for me, those records gave a lift to my imagination that nothing else provided. I was amused by "K-K-K-Katie" and "When Father Papered the Parlour," and cried as I listened to the mournful ballad called "The Baggage Coach Ahead."

Mother, not one to cry easily, could drop a tear or two for "The Letter Edged in Black" and "After the Ball."

My favourite was "Marching Through Georgia." Undaunted by its foreign roots, I would put that record on, wind up the gramophone, and march endlessly around the tiny living-room like a real trooper. I even whittled a wooden gun to add a touch of reality to the charade. Poor mother. With the First War only fifteen years behind her, she had no stomach for such parades. And had she known that soon I would carry a real rifle off to war, my playing soldier would have sparked distress. As it was, she merely said, "This isn't Georgia, so you can stop your marchin'." I'd go back to "papering the parlour."

When we lost our home, our parents miraculously hung on to the gramophone. And while we were off in the bush camp in 1936, it waited for us in a mean little house which my parents had rented on the outskirts of Huntsville. Then Fate took over.

My brother had a bad case of sinus infection in the logging camp. There was nothing for him but a long ride to town on a sidecar of the railway. He and a chum took off in the night, and we didn't see them again until camp broke up two weeks later. And guess what? My brother, always the "man about town," had managed to get Dad's old car going, and had spent his nights cruising Huntsville's main street with his buddy! And what did he use for money? Why, he had sold

Dad's fine bellows camera, which had been our sole record of family history for years. It was my Dad's only treasure. And, as if to add insult to injury, he had also relieved us of our beloved gramophone, complete with all the records!

I never quite forgave my brother for that.

He Shoots! He Scores!

During the thirties, rural life in Muskoka was a tough experience. Most families struggled to eke out an existence by working in the bush or by combatting the rocky environment to cultivate their precious patches of soil. Those were the years of the "Great Depression," and even the seasonal flow of tourists from the south had dwindled to a trickle.

"Times are tough," was my mother's laconic description of what, for her, was enough to test the very soul. Even so, my brother Vernon and I fared quite well. We had our precious old dog, Jumbo, two cows, a flock of chickens, some turkeys—and Jimmie and Jamie, two pigs which I counted as friends. We had school and chores, of course; but we were free from worry, and we always had enough to eat and wear. Except for the odd attack of whooping cough or the croup, life for us was a great adventure.

It was less adventurous for our parents. There was little to lift the spirit above the daily tedium of work and worry. Even so, the rural community wove itself together with barn dances, card parties, quilting bees and the odd school concert. But they were infrequent events indeed, and when they occurred they took on a glow that went well beyond the ordinary. Even visiting a neighbouring farm was an adventure—especially if it involved the whole family. One such visit is with me yet.

It was a Saturday afternoon in December, and Vernon and I had just finished drawing wood with our dog Jumbo. As we hung his harness in the shed and swept the snow from our clothes, Mother called us inside.

"Now the two of you get undressed, ready for your baths. I've got the water already hot and the wash-tub is waiting for you. I want you to hurry, because we're goin' somewhere special tonight."

"Where are we goin'?" asked Vernon.

"Never mind. I'm not tellin' you just yet. But you're doin' such a good job haulin' that wood, your dad and me think it's time for a treat. Besides, we've been invited. Now get into that tub, Vernon, and don't splash water all over the floor."

Ordinarily the Saturday night bath was a gruelling experience for us, about on par with berry-picking. But with only the tub between us and a mysterious adventure, the ordeal was almost pleasant. In half the usual time we were into the water and out again, ready for action.

"Now will you tell us where we are goin'?" begged Vernon.

"We're goin' to the Bunns'."

Our faces fell. Going to the Bunns' was an infrequent event, the novelty of which was dulled by the fact that the reason was always the same as a visit to the Darlings'—to play cards. It was worse than a visit to the Darlings', because there were no children at the Bunns'. To go there for the mail was one thing. But to go there for nothing was no fun at all.

"Aw, who wants to go to old Bunns' for a game of cards?" Vernon's question was rhetorical.

"We're not going to play cards," Dad answered.

"Then why're we goin'?"

"You'll see. Now come along. We're going to walk. It's only a mile."

Early that evening I stood in the Bunn kitchen and faced the wonder of the age. It was a radio. It sat on a special table by the post office pigeon holes, and was connected by wires to batteries that sat on a shelf beneath. Chairs had been placed in front of it, and the fine lace runner on which it sat gave the whole arrangement the appearance of a religious altar. It was the Bunns' newest possession, and they had generously invited the Dennis family to share its advent.

It was the first time that I had seen a radio. Of course I knew about them, had even heard my father talking about getting one some day. But this was the first time I had seen one. Already the trip to the Bunns' was worthwhile.

The occasion, of course, was not to look at the radio, but to listen to it; and not to hear just anything, but to hear what most Canadians of the mid-thirties would consider the most important program that the radio had to offer—Foster Hewitt's National Hockey broadcast. Vernon and I knew all about the National Hockey League, of course. Even without a radio, we, like our compatriots, had an embryonic pride in our national game; and although our experience was completely vicarious, we had gleaned enough from newspapers, team calendars, and adult talk to have our favourite players, and looked forward to one day having our own skates, pucks and sticks. We had played at the game on the road, using sticks cut from the bush and frozen horse manure for a puck. But we never had seen a real game, and certainly never heard one broadcast.

"We don't turn it on until it's time for the game," explained Arthur Bunn, the adult son. "Saves the batteries that way. Take chairs up here where you can hear. Can you hear alright from over there, Father?"

"Har'arumph." Apparently Silas Bunn could hear alright from his chair by the stove. Finally Arthur turned a switch. A dial in the centre of the radio's face glowed a dull orange, and a crackling hum announced that it was alive. Then, with a magic sound that raised goose pimples on my neck the radio spoke.

"Hello Canada, and hockey fans in the United States and Newfoundland." It was Foster Hewitt.

For the next two hours I sat entranced as the voice in this magic box brought hockey heroes right in to the Bunn kitchen, with its infectious description of their play. Naturally, my heroes were all players for the Toronto Maple Leafs, and I gradually relaxed enough to listen for their names. King Clancy, Charlie Conacher, Ace Bailey and George Hainsworth all came alive that night for me, thanks to Foster Hewitt, the Bunns, and whoever invented the radio. I was not alone that night. It was 1933, the dawn of the National Hockey broadcast, and thousands of native sons were equally enthralled. Before the decade was over, Foster Hewitt's broadcast, with his excited call, "He shoots! He scores!" would bind Canadians with a unique cultural bond, more romantic than any other at the time. Even the women, so traditionally separated from the interests of men, were united with their husbands in the excitement of the game; and Mother was heard to comment, "That Bailey should just give that Shore a good smack" as she reacted to Foster's graphic description of her favourite being dumped. Even if he had heard her, Ace Bailey could not have responded. He lay on the ice with a fractured skull!

The evening ended with coffee and cookies, and a cold walk home. But the memory of it lingered in my mind. It must have dallied in the minds of our parents, too, for the next day I heard them say that a family really shouldn't be without a radio. "Maybe next year," said Mother, the brand-new fan of Foster Hewitt—and the stricken Ace Bailey.

Christmas Memories

My eyes tended to enlarge with the thought of Christmas; and the usual parental admonitions that "Santa Claus won't be able to afford much this year" fell upon deaf ears. After all, he brought me that big truck last year, didn't he? And it must have cost a fortune! Anyway, I could always dream.

I was not alone. Soon after the spooks of Hallowe'en retreated with the darkness, the magic of Christmas crept into our school. You couldn't see it at first. But you knew that it was there when bits of evidence began to herald its coming.

The snow became deeper as we trudged to school, and the teacher began to take an unusual interest in our ability to recite and to speak out clearly. Then, when she announced that there would be a Christmas concert, certain ordinary pupils were converted into Biblical characters and the rest of us repeatedly stood on the tiny stage to hone our renditions of trusted Christmas favourites.

One day we were instructed to bring a comb and tissue paper to school. And then, by some new magic, we put paper to comb and hummed our way all the way through "O Little Town of Bethlehem" and "Jolly Old St. Nicholas." Clyde and I, judged to be less melodious than the others, were deprived of our tissue papers but allowed to remain in the band as long as we promised not to make a sound.

I didn't mind. My claim to fame would come at the concert with the recitation of a verse, which began like this:

> One hundred years ago today,
> The wilderness was here;
> The man with powder in his gun
> Went out to hunt the deer.
> But now the thing has changed somewhat,
> Into another plan—
> The deer with powder on her face,
> Goes out to hunt the man!

Then one of us sought to capture the audience by renditions of a song, popular at the time. It was called "When the Work's All Done This Fall" and went like this:

> A group of jolly cowboys,
> Discussing plans at ease
> Says one, I'll tell you something, boys,

If you will listen please.
I am an old cowpuncher.
And though I'm dressed in rags,
I used to be a tough one, boys,
And go on great big jags
But I have got a home, boys,
A good one, you all know
Though I've not seen that home, boys,
Since long, long ago
But I'm going back to Dixie
Once more to see them all,
And I'm going to see my mother, boys,
When the work's all done this fall.

There was more, but the above provides a taste of what the Ullswater audience could expect at the concert. (And readers would have been deprived of even this except for the kind assistance of Rosemarie Freeman, a friend who found the song in her archives and sharpened my memory!)

Art lessons, too, announced that Christmas was coming, as we became devoted to the making of decorations for the tree. I remember the arduous task of making the cardboard stars, covering them with paste and sprinkling them with silver dust more suitable for wedding cakes. Long garland ropes were fashioned from strips of red, white and green tissue paper linked together into loops; and coloured paper was crunched into balls to occupy prominent places on the tree when it arrived. Our creative teacher even showed us how to cut eye-catchers from the Eaton's catalogue. Surely, our tree would not want for decorative finery!

At last we were ready for the tree. After threshing about in the deepest of the woods surrounding our school, we emerged triumphant. Cut to size, and midst much conflicting advice about its proper display, it finally found its place in the corner. Armed with our decorations, we attacked it with glee; and when we were finished, it exuded a beauty and aroma that were unmistakably Christmas. The tree was ready. We were ready, and when the nearby farmer came over to hang the curtains on the stage the teacher was ready, too. The concert was a week away. Then a personal disaster struck.

The Bunn farm was the designated post office for Ullswater, and one of my daily duties was to stop by and pick up the mail for the Dennis family. There was never much to pick up, really. Perhaps a letter from Aunt Louise, who lived out west, or a letter from my cousin Ruth. But on most occasions I came away empty-handed.

But one December day just before the concert, I stopped by and picked up a small parcel! I could hardly wait to get home and watch Mother open it. When I got to the house, Mother was nowhere to be seen. I called out but there was no answer. I checked the stable and hen-house. No sign of Mother. I returned to the kitchen and looked at the little parcel on the table. What should a boy do in such circumstances? Why, he should help his mother, of course. She would be busy enough, getting supper ready and all. The least I could do was open this parcel for her. Which I promptly did.

Mother had gone over to Beathune's to borrow some sugar. When she came home, there was her son Lloyd, happily playing on the floor. In front of him sat a cardboard cut-out complete with a tiny stage on which sat a tiger and a lion. And Lloyd? Why he was taking aim at the lion with a little gun, loaded with a cork! "Bang!" he said as he pulled the trigger. The lion disappeared from the stage.

"Lloyd!" his mother fairly shouted, "What are you doin'? Where'd you get that?"

"Look Mom!" I said excitedly. "I got this in the mail! Isn't it just dandy? Came with three corks, too!"

With one swift motion, she gathered the treasures from the floor and swept them out of sight. Then I was on the receiving end of a stern lecture about opening the King's Mail when it wasn't addressed to me. As a punishment, she took a stick to me. Midst plaintive sobs, I promised never to do it again.

At last the magic night of the concert arrived. By some supernatural power, the school expanded to accommodate everyone in Ullswater. The makeshift curtain pulled open repeatedly to reveal one "celebrity" after another, as we, like trained seals, paraded our skills before admiring parents.Then, just before coffee and sandwiches, Santa Claus burst through the door, and with much laughter and poor pronunciation, he distributed gifts to all of us.

"I know where they come from," Marjorie announced to me. "They come from the Women's Institute. And you know what else? My dad's the Santa Claus."

I didn't mind. I received a colouring book, and it was the real thing. And as far as I was concerned, so was Santa Claus.

The tree that came alive each year at our house was always something special. We were poor, but by some magic our parents had managed to assemble ornaments that delighted the eye. There was a furry monkey, several ornate balls and a number of tiny trinkets to give variety. And, to give a touch of personal glory to it all, my rattle hung proudly in the top-most branch. Even today the rattle, the monkey, and a few of the other ornaments like them take their positions annually to remind me of those good old days.

Christmas presents, on the other hand, were far less conspicuous. Apart from Santa's moment of madness one year when he left me a beautiful big truck, gifts were a scarce commodity during the thirties.

But we had grown used to this circumstance and were happy to receive whatever Santa managed to leave. A pair of leather mitts or leather-topped rubbers made one feel quite grown up. And if a toy managed to find a place under our tree, I was especially delighted. A top, a game of Snakes and Ladders, or Tiddley Winks, a set of building blocks, even games of Old Maid and The Lost Heir had presented themselves in the past.

And I'll never forget the beautiful tractor; with real rubber treads!

Books were high on my list of wishes: *The Boy Allies with Haig in Flanders*, *The Pony Rider Boys in the Ozark Mountains*, and any books written by Horatio Alger were welcome at my house. One year Aunt

Flossie sent me a book called *Grace Harlow in the High Sierras*. It was really meant for girls, but I read it anyway.

But those were other times. This year, I had robbed the King's Mail and even though I'd been punished, and said I was sorry, Santa might have struck me from his list for being naughty. I would soon find out. When Christmas morning arrived, I found that Santa had left me with a shooting game complete with cardboard animal targets and a pop-gun with three corks! I played with them all day. Unknown to me, of course, was the fact that my mother had saved endless Shredded Wheat box tops in order to send away for my present, which I had illegally opened in the mail.

I began to suspect that Mother and Santa Claus were in cahoots with each other. If so, I thought it was a good relationship. At least I was still on the list.

One Christmas adventure in the 1930s began with turkeys. On an earlier trip to Huntsville, Mother arranged with Mr. Ginsberg, owner of the Huntsville Trading Company, to deliver a dozen dressed birds on the day before Christmas. All fall, the turkey flock had received special attention and, apart from a few which fell victim to raiding foxes, the birds grew to fulfill the promise of Christmas delivery and dollars for the Dennis purse.

Death to the turkeys was dealt two days before Christmas with Dad slitting their throats, Mother drawing out their insides, and Vernon and I plucking them nude.

For me, the unpleasant job was made more attractive by the satisfaction of plucking Old Pete, a particularly ferocious gobbler that had given me uncomfortable moments during feeding. Killed and clean, the turkeys were hung by their feet in the shed, ready for their last ride.

Fortunately, the full blast of winter had not yet hit the district, and since the roads were plowed we were able to take the car to town. With Vernon and I sharing the back seat with the twelve turkeys, we headed for Huntsville.

A Christmas visit to town had extraordinary delights to offer a country boy. The first to present itself was the bustle of Main Street, the excitement of which was all the more striking after the silence of the country road. Its sights and sounds swept deliciously over us as Dad manoeuvered the Ford into traffic.

Everyone seemed to have converged upon Huntsville on this last shopping day before Christmas, and, since main street was the shopping centre of the district, it was the focal point of attention. It was also the route of through traffic, and gave itself up to shoppers and travellers alike.

Cars and cutters jockeyed for position with sleighs and logging trucks, while pedestrians slopped along the slushy sidewalks, making sporadic darts through traffic to the opposite sides of the street. Breathing life into it all were the discordant sounds of motors and horses, and shouts of direction and greeting, made melodious by the tinkling of bells that were the trademark of sleighs in winter. And over it all floated the sweet notes of the Salvation Army band, giving meaning to the festive mood of the town.

Main Street traffic was merely the overture. The great delight lay in its stores, which were especially entrancing at Christmas. Their lights had a different lustre, somehow; and their goods had a new allure that came with a dash of red ribbon and tinsel. We were conscious enough of our strained circumstances to realize that the treasures were unattainable, of course, even with the help of Santa Claus.

Still, one never knew what might happen at such a magic time, and although I knew enough not to ask for anything, I allowed myself to hope that at least one of the stores' delights would find its way to my house.

After the turkey transaction had been made, Mother escorted me to Eaton's Department Store. There, on the second floor, I found myself in the presence of the great man himself! Santa sat on a makeshift throne, and without even writing it down, took my order for a new truck. He seemed pleased with the idea.

"Now you and Vernon take this dollar and go shoppin' by yourselves," said Mother. "Maybe you can find a present for each other.

Meet us at Wardell's store in an hour. And don't waste that money on candy."

Off we went, proud of our sudden purchasing power. A brief conference resulted in our resolve to forgo presents for ourselves in favour of gifts for our Mother. In no time at all the dollar was exchanged for a milk pitcher and a large wooden spoon, which Vernon insisted were just the things for a good cook like Mother. And we had enough left over to buy a plug of chewing tobacco for Dad.

By the time we got to Wardell's, I found that Santa had gone there too. There he was, on another throne, just like the one at Eaton's! Taking no chances, I paid my second visit, repeated my order, and was surprised that he gave me no hint of recognition, and greeted my request for a truck as quite a novel idea!

Christmas Eve was no time for families to be wandering the roads, and as evening approached I was pleased to see that our parents prepared to leave for home. With mysterious parcels packed about our feet, we bundled into the cold car and headed for Ullswater. With luck, we would be safely in our bed in plenty of time for Santa to go about his business undisturbed.

As we headed into the darkness beyond the town, it became clear that the ride home would not be without difficulty. In no time at all, the windows of the car were frosted over, and the view outside was lost to us.

"Looks like it's going to be a rough trip," muttered Dad as he furiously rubbed the windshield with his mitt.

He peeked through the tiny place that he had cleared, and watched as it quickly frosted over again to hide the road from view. Rub, squint, and rub again; our father seemed destined to spend the trip with one hand on the wheel and the other on the windshield. Soon Mother joined the fight, vigorously rubbing away at the blinding frost. There was really nothing unusual about the frosted car windows. The Ford had no heater, and once the family boarded the car on a cold winter day, Mother Nature usually reacted by coating the windows. As a defence, Dad sometimes lit a candle and stuck it on the dashboard to warm the glass. Even rubbing the windshield with camphor would fight the frost—if one had the presence of mind to equip himself. On this occasion, Dad was lacking both candle and camphor. Rubbing and scraping would have to do. To make matters worse, a fine snow had begun to fall, making it difficult to see more than a few yards beyond the car.

"Gee, Dad," I complained, "At this rate we'll never get home, it will be so late Santa will be gone, and he won't leave anything, because he'll think nobody lives at our house."

"Stop your grumblin'," said Mother. "We'll be home when we get there."

"There ain't no Santa Claus, anyway, so what are you worried about?" My brother was five years older than I.

"There is too," I countered. "Saw him at Eaton's, and Wardell's too."

Thankfully, Vernon didn't press the matter. Beyond asking me how Santa Claus could be in two places at once, he let it drop.

It was already past ten o'clock. It would be long after midnight before we got home. Christmas Eve would be over before we even got to sleep.

Sure enough, we arrived home to find our tree bereft of gifts. Santa must have come and gone, and, finding us not at home, left nothing. While Dad stoked the fire in the box-stove, I hurried up the stairs and huddled under the covers, willing sleep to come. There was still a chance, if we all got to sleep, that he would come, after all. For the longest time, Vernon and I lay listening to our parents downstairs amid muffled sounds of conversation and rustling paper. In exasperation, I went to the top of the stairs and pleaded with them.

"Can't you come to bed and leave the groceries till morning?" I asked. "There's still a chance, you know."

"There'll be no chance at all if you don't go to sleep. We'll be along in a minute."

Finally the adventure of the long day slipped mercifully from my senses, the rustling of the paper ceased, and I was asleep.

Early Christmas morning two weary parents were rudely jolted from their sleep by the clanging bell of a fire truck. Gleaming red, and with ladders poised, it suddenly appeared over their heads, clutched in the hands of its proud owner.

"Look, Mom and Dad! Wake up! Look at this! It was under the tree! And there's other stuff there, too, lots and lots of stuff. He must have come, after all! Come on downstairs and see!"

With feigned surprise, my parents admired the truck so suddenly thrust upon them, and realizing that further peace was impossible, prepared to go downstairs and view the miracle for themselves.

"Vernon, start the fire in the cookstove, and both of you get washed and dressed, and help your dad with the chores while I fix breakfast, then we'll see what else is under that tree."

The "what else" turned out to be assorted articles of clothing, a real hockey stick and puck for Vernon, together with a pair of horse-hide mitts, a game of Snakes and Ladders, the pitcher and wooden spoon, and the plug of tobacco.

It wasn't much, but on that Christmas of 1934 it was a cornucopia of delight, made even more remarkable by the events of the night before.

One thing was missing.

The candy dish which Mother had so carefully filled with chocolates the night before, now sat empty beneath the tree. And stretched out by the box-stove was the thief, licking his snout with obscene satisfaction.

"Jumbo, you ate those chocolates!" accused Vernon. "You old pig! I could smash you into smithereens!"

"Never mind," said Mother. "I suppose he has to have Christmas too. Anyway, I've got some more."

May Days

Spring has sprung,
The grass is riz,
I wonder where
The flowers is?

That tiresome ditty was on the lips of every child—and not a few adults—when I was a country child in Muskoka. The signs were everywhere; and although they were ages old, there was something new about them every year. Gradually the days got longer, until you could get your chores done and still see the ball well enough to play Auntie-High Over.

The snow banks would slip away to become rivulets in the ditches, and fill the ruts on the road. The first courageous trees would tentatively shoot out their buds, and the dead sod would, almost overnight, offer a green carpet to cover the fields. Finally, you would know that it had arrived when the first bouquet of snowdrops and hepaticas appeared on the teacher's desk. Within a week, she would be deluged with an array of offerings that included everything from dog-toothed violets to dutchman's breeches. Following a ritual as old as childhood itself, we would raid the forest glens in search of the best violets, trilliums and wild lilies we could find, and all the while we were never quite sure why we did it. Perhaps it was the smell of the newborn growth; maybe it was the subtle suggestion of beauty that attracted us. Whatever the root of the ritual, we were party to it, and swept the forest with unaccustomed verve.

One plant was a pariah. It was the country leek, and only the bravest of boys would pick it. Then, if he went all the way and actually ate its delicious white root on the way to school—well, his colleagues seventy years later would call him "really cool!" Back then, we'd just say that there was trouble waiting ahead.

The leek, proud symbol of Wales and delectable member of the onion family, offered one problem. The consumer of its smooth white root would exude an odour so offensive that even the most sensitive teacher would back away. Then, true to the admonition on her certificate, she would mete out such punishment as would break the bravest boy. I remember Vernon and his friend Myron facing the wrath of Miss McNeilly one spring day in 1933. She ordered them to go home for the remainder of the day. Worse still, she denied them the right to the blackboard brushes for the rest of the month. Everyone knew that cleaning the brushes was about as good as it could get. But such breaches of decorum were not taken lightly, and only a heedless jackass would fail to get the message.

As beautiful and bountiful as spring was, it had a dark side too. Only Mother Nature herself could enjoy watching people in our part of the world suddenly begin to slap themselves silly with the advent of warm weather. The culprits, of course, were the insects that joined us in the rites of spring. By the millions they came, blackflies, sandflies, moths, mosquitoes, June bugs, lady bugs, houseflies, bees, hornets, and countless other pests.

When we complained of the torment offered by those invaders, my mother would say "What you gain in the meat, you lose in the potatoes," which, roughly translated, meant that one can't expect everything about spring to be bright and beautiful. But she suffered with the rest of us; and I can see her yet, taking in the wash with swarms of mosquitoes about her head. Some of us, vainly trying to put a positive spin on things, would try to impress our friends by letting a mosquito drink her fill on our arms before crushing her with a sudden slap. The resulting blotch of blood was supposed to impress the onlooker, but I don't recall any applause following my act of bravado.

The pests were particularly bad in the evening, and on sultry days. Our school had no screens, and many homes were also poorly equipped in that regard. Smudge fires were a common weapon of defence, especially if fishing or working in the garden. Citronella was a common defence against insects, but one never seemed to be able to rub it in the right places. Fortunately, its lemon-like aroma had a positive effect upon the wearer, if not the invader.

In the home, mother used fly coils and the occasional sticky pad to capture the careless houseflies. These devices were of no use in the outbuildings, however, and many a docile beast was driven into frenzied torment by various kinds of flies. A swishing tail was a paltry weapon indeed when attacked by hordes of insects, each bearing a sting capable of severe discomfort. Even animals in the wild fell victim to these attacks, and there were stories of great, elegant beasts being driven mad by the endless onslaught of blackflies. For hundreds of miles they ranged during their brief attack upon all flesh in the animal kingdom—which, unfortunately, included all the human beings in Muskoka. Why, even our teacher, so immune from all things ordinary, was fair game in fly season.

As children, one of our most dramatic insect enemies was the wasp, or hornet. Asleep in its grey nest, it was no problem. But we were seldom wise enough to leave well enough alone. Long after spring had come and gone, some young unfortunate could be seen dashing from the bush with the enemy swarming around him in hot pursuit. In such crises, we often shopped in Mother Nature's store for a soothing balm. Mud or cow manure would be applied to the affected parts. In such emergencies, the source of the relief was a minor detail.

One group most afflicted were the men of the district who worked the forest. For some reason, the time for stripping the hemlock of its bark coincided with the blackfly season. A warm job, requiring considerable exertion, it was best done with the sleeves rolled up as if to invite additional torture. The day was long, the work hard, and the bark a hot marketing item of the day. Nearby lay a great tannery in Huntsville, eagerly waiting to devour each slab of tan bark that came its way. Stripping bark put bread on the table, and no man worth his salt would let a few million blackflies get in his way. No sir!

Naturally, we young people never gave a thought to the discomfort of our elders during fly season. We were busy enough with our own world. Among the adventures that occupied our minds as May progressed was the shedding of clothing. Long underwear was the first to go in the boys' world. This was followed by abandoning breeks and high rubbers for overalls and running shoes. Then it was a race to be the first of the season to go barefoot. Following that endurance test, another race ensued. The lake, so thickly covered with ice all winter, now gave up the ghost and waved its frigid invitation to "come on in!" Gingerly we would summon the will to face the daunting challenge. Suddenly, someone would shout "Last one in's a monkey's uncle!" I had that dubious honour more than once. Then it was back to school on Tuesday.

Why Tuesday, you ask. Because, on the previous Friday we had gathered up all our courage to sing:

> The twenty-fourth of May
> Is the Queen's birthday—
> If you don't give us a holiday
> We'll all run away!

Queen Victoria was long dead—but she came back to life for one day each year—on our school calendar.

The Devil Made Us Do It

In our home everybody worked—Mother, Dad, Vernon, Lloyd—even Jumbo and Jessie had their appointed tasks in those far-off days of the Depression. It wasn't just because we were poor. It was the thing one did, the custom, the proper thing; and I can still remember my mother's overworked admonition, "The Devil finds work for idle hands!" Since I'd rather be caught dead than work for the Devil, I did what I was told. Our house at Ullswater was a good example. When I got up in the morning, I could be reasonably assured that the day would be filled with tedious, tasteless, torturous tasks that were really inspired by Satan himself. By the time I had cleaned out the stable and fed Jessie and the cows, I could hear Mother calling. "Don't forget to feed the chickens—and check for eggs while you're there." And of course by this time I'd be sliding into the pig-pen to be greeted with further orders from our pigs, Jimmy and Jamie. "How about some slop from the kitchen, you little whippersnapper?" they seemed to say with their guttural grunts. Back in the house, I'd be greeted with the order to go back outside and clean off my rubbers, which always acted like magnets to capture every bit of odious evidence of where I had been.

"And while you're out there take this pail and bring fresh water from the well. Land's sakes! Do I have to tell you everything to do around here?" Mother's exclamation was born more out of habit than frustration. She was a busy woman, and it was just her way of reminding her son of the realities of life, lest he forget. I took it for what it was worth.

So did my brother Vernon. Being a sibling, he was subjected to the same rules as I. But being five years older, he performed his tasks according to the universal rule of nature: "Don't do what you can coerce your younger brother into doing." I was the low man on the totem pole; and, short of a miraculous reversal of ages, there was nothing I could do about it. By now, it would be eight o'clock, time I had those fifteen jobs already done with a little help from Vernon—and now I had barely time to wash my hands, clean my teeth and comb my hair before heading up the road to an even more notorious sweat-shop called a school. There, the teacher would greet you with a prim propriety that was about as far removed from your pig-pen as you could get. But she, too, knew about chores. The road into the unknown was dotted with extra-curricular tasks that were part of the price to pay for the privilege of going to school. In actual fact, these tasks were often welcomed by the slaves as brief tickets to freedom. Whether they were performed within or beyond school hours, they were usually accepted with an alacrity that would disappoint the Devil, the author of all slave labour. Cleaning brushes was high on the list of welcome tasks. One got to go outside, and beat the Devil out of the school wall; and the harder you worked at it, the better you felt, somehow. It was a kind of jail-house therapy, and the one doing it always felt a sense of deprivation when it was over. I've been convinced in later years that those brushes received more abuse through cleaning than through use.

Then there were the boards to clean, the ink-wells and water-pail to fill, and wood to get for the stove; and as for planting flowers—at school it was fun, at home it was a real chore.

When we got home after school there they all were, ready and waiting. It was as if that old Devil had destroyed all the good works done by the slaves in the morning and created new ones to welcome us home. Feed the chickens, feed the pigs, feed the horse, feed the cows—and milk them too, if Dad's not home. Thus, just as I was about to drop from exhaustion, I'd hear "Lloyd, split some kindling and, oh yes, the lamps need fillin'. Have you got any homework? Vernon, you're the boss. See that your brother gets them things done, you hear?" Vernon heard—and I got the things done.

Every season had its own burdens, of course. With Spring came the job of making syrup and sugar, and later, the annual battle of the garden. This latter was a bittersweet experience. On the one hand, we welcomed the end of the wearisome winter; but on the other hand, we dreaded the endless hoeing, raking and planting. And just when we thought that we'd done everything possible to that piece of ground, up would come another jungle of growth, just begging to be cared for all summer. I'd hoe and hoe, and pick everything in sight; and just when my fingers were about to drop off, Dad would tell me to get a can and pick those bugs off the potato plants.

Fall was worse. Now the potatoes had to be dug up, along with the turnips, the carrots, the cabbages and the beets, and put away for winter. Into the root-house they would go along with the jams and jellies, and other jarred delights.

The chore that I detested most of all made its debut in the spring. During the warm days of June the berry blossoms would give way to fruit, just waiting for a boy's eager fingers to pluck them. I didn't actually mind picking the odd berry on my way to school; but when Mother tied a pail to her apron, I sought a place to hide! That pail spelled trouble. But she would seek me out, and, with the sound of excitement in her voice, she would say, "Come on Lloyd, we're goin' berry-pickin'. Here's your pail; bring that basket, too. It's got sandwiches and cold tea for our lunch."

That latter announcement meant that I was in for a full day of doing a job that I absolutely hated. We would begin with an attack on the strawberries; then, as the summer moved along, we would advance to the fences which bordered upon the raspberries and gooseberries. By August, we would be well into the Blueberry Campaign, having briefly skirmished with the Blackberry Battalion. Finally, just before school opened, I was relieved of my pail and allowed to retreat, leaving Mother to clean and lock up the captive fruit in jars, ready for their place in the root-house. It was a relief to return to school and clean those brushes.

I exaggerate, of course. The berry attacks didn't take all summer. They were sporadic rather than an all-out, two-month war. But they were a significant part of the slavery that I felt subjected to in the world of childhood work called "chores."

A story more apocryphal than true, grew over the years. It went like this:

Bessie and her son Lloyd were out picking berries one day when a big black bear rose to confront them.

"Run and get your dad," said Bessie. Lloyd ran home and told his dad Alf, who ran back with Lloyd, carrying his gun. When they arrived on the scene, there was the bear, still glaring at Bessie who stood, hands on hips, glaring right back.

"What are you going to do, Dad?" asked Lloyd.

"Nothing," answered Alf. "The bear got himself into this mess. Let him find a way out of it."

It may not be true, but the story reveals a lot about that indomitable berry-picker, better known as my mother.

Those Good Old Golden Rule Days

Tradition called them "schools." But we knew better. They were really fortresses where children gathered daily to ward off the evils of Ignorance. They were cultural necessities, those towers of knowledge, and some were mighty in their majesty. But most were rural outposts, strung like beads on a necklace across the land. Their commanders were unheralded, but these young leaders led the charge with a zeal that far out-shone their meager salaries. Most of them were women. It's of passing interest that in the nine "outposts" where I served as a young warrior, only three were men (two, if I only counted the good ones). Each day, with the regulations of the Education Act firmly embedded in their minds, they would leave their lodgings, and head for the one-roomed schools, undaunted by the task that lay ahead.

And so would we. We were conscripts, to be sure. But since it was in our best interest to serve, we went more or less willingly. Day after day we would hear the sound of the bell that tolled from the roof of the ramparts. Like bugs, we would creep along from all directions across the landscape, until we reached our goal. All shapes and sizes were we, and bundled according to the weather. We carried lunch pails and school bags, and assorted paraphernalia meant to serve the cause. And just as our legs were about to give out, we reached the school.

And it was ready for us. Its floors were swept, its boards were clean, and the blinds were a uniform height. The box-stove exuded a welcome heat, the pail had been filled with water from the spring across the road, and the coat-hooks were bare and inviting. To top it off, a pail-a-day toilet had been installed, ready to invite the inexperienced to savour the pleasure of indoor relief.

We were a motley crew, and as we removed our coats we revealed our true selves. Some were like dainty dolls, far too fragile for the trials ahead. Others seemed almost in need of a shave, already veterans of this annual war. But as the magic hour of nine approached, we were as one against the enemy when we stood in five neat rows before the teacher. She, too, was ready and waiting and, in flawless script, had already written six exercises on the blackboard. Above them all was the date "Monday, February 10, 1934." Let the battle begin!

Lest we required a boost of patriotism, our charge into the fray was preceded by the singing of "God Save the King." Indeed, pictures of King George v and Queen Mary hung on the wall facing us, separated by a framed Canadian coat-of-arms, marking our country's sixtieth anniversary, 1867-1927. The anthem was followed by the Lord's Prayer and a reading of scripture.

"Take your seats," ordered the teacher.

Our desks were in rows, screwed to the floor. In older outposts, the seats held a crew of two; but they had been gradually replaced by singles, which came in two sizes. An ink-well sat in the upper right corner, which was replenished as required from an ink-pot at the front. There were no desks with ink-wells on the left, reminding left-handers like me that this war was to be fought with the right hand.

At the front, on a small stage, was the command post. The teacher's desk drawer contained two important weapons of war: the Register and the strap. The first was in daily use, and appeared immediately after we sat down. It recorded our presence or absence; and truly, it was the finest example of penmanship in the community. And well it might be, for it was the first to be judged by the Inspector when he made his rounds.

The strap was intended to put the "fear of the Lord" in young miscreants, should they flag in their duty; and it was a mark of pride to suffer the strap without flinching. A more frequent "adjuster" was on the blackboard ledge. It was the pointer. It visited my knuckles upon occasion for the crime of being left-handed. (Its visits were fruitless, however, since I am still of that persuasion.)

In the corner at the right stood the library, which was really a modest cupboard. It was crowned with a globe, and held about fifty books. A rolled-up map of the world hung over the blackboard, and its Neilson's chocolate-bar islands revealed its source.

The cupboard in the opposite corner held the school's supplies. Built on a grander scale, it was the "quartermaster's stores" for the young band of warriors, and held a veritable treasure of tools for teaching and learning. Paste, and paper in mats, sheets and strips vied for space with rulers, pens and their precious nibs. Workbooks, complete with multiplication tables, were thrust upon the warriors. Exercise books sporting finer paper were available as our skills developed with the pen. And there was a handwriting book that showed us what acceptable writing was all about, complete with exercises designed to develop our skills. And pencils! Those yellow hordes were grasped by grubby hands and worked their way to a grinding death in the pencil-sharpener on the window-sill. Truly, it was not a healthy place for pencils. And many of the marks that they did make were rubbed out by erasers provided by the cupboard. One was dual purpose, soft grey on one end, and red on the opposite; the other looked like a cube of brown sugar. Soft and crumbly, it went by the title "art gum."

Chalk came packed in sawdust, 144 pieces to the box, both white and coloured. Like the pencils, those sticks were doomed to disappear. But during their lives, they made strange and wonderful marks on the blackboard, only to be regularly wiped out by the brushes. Their last traces were seen on the school's outside wall, where eager young monitors beat the brushes clean.

Plasticine came in grey, green, red, yellow and black. And scissors?

There they were, right beside the paints and crayons. Sticks and yarn, needles and thread, the list went on and on. And all these supplies for war were provided by the Ontario Government, courtesy of the local three-man School Board. What the Board did not provide were our pencil boxes, which came in different shapes, and often reflected the means of the owner. I yearned for the two-tiered style which swung open, and had a sliding lid. But my simple box with its hinged lid served me well.

The text books were the essential weaponry of the outpost's arsenal. They were designed to ward off the severest wounds caused by Ignorance, and ranged from language to literature. The largest was the Canadian Public School Geography, and the most relentless was the Spelling Book, which was the basic weapon used throughout the campaign. There were books on Arithmetic, Composition and Grammar, Canadian History, British History and Civics. Indeed, there was little chance, if the young soldiers used their weapons well, for Ignorance to survive! For me, the Readers were the best, the most reliable, and the most engaging of the lot. They were a family of five—Primer, First, Second, Third and Fourth books, and offered a progressive deluge of everything from simple verse to engaging story and serious admonition. The Primer offered opening fire by quoting R.L. Stephenson:

> Happy Hearts and Happy Faces
> Happy Play in grassy places—
> That is how in ancient ages,
> Children grew to kings and sages.

Opening page, First Book revealed:

> Little drops of water
> Little grains of sand
> Make the mighty ocean,
> And the pleasant land.

Little deeds of kindness,
Little words of love,
Make our earth an Eden,
Like the Heavens above.

The Second Book opened with the National Anthem and followed immediately with the fable about the Arab and the camel. Its closing shot was "Abide With Me."

Grey Cup fans would be pleased to know that the Third Book began with an admonition about Empire Day by the Governor General, Earl Grey. More than 100 titles were fired off on 340 pages before this weapon was fully discharged with its final shot, "In Flanders Fields."

Fourth Book was a cannon. About twenty titles dealt with combat, either in prose or verse, and an equal number stirred the patriotic spirit. My favourite was called "Canadians, Canadians—That's All!", a stirring tale of a glorious engagement near Ypres during the First World War.

The Fourth Reader was a catalogue of British-Canadian literature, and for many of us, it provided a most effective and engaging getaway into the land of enlightenment—and, as it turned out, the world of war.

And so, on any given day the world could look in upon the young teacher leading her charges armed with the tools of education and her own imaginative effort. To the casual observer, the task may have seemed simple. After all, there were only sixteen of us, and most of us were smaller than she. Not so obvious however was the fact that we ranged in age from six to sixteen upon occasion, and we were all a mixture of varying levels of ability and interest. Success or failure largely depended upon her ability to keep us all actively engaged in our separate activities at the same time. It required the skill of a juggler, the art of the magician. And Miss Card had both.

"Coreen, will you please give Grant and Ivan the mats and strips and get them started on weaving their mats. Harvey, Clyde and

Lloyd, please do the arithmetic exercise 95 on page 88. Eileen and Edith, please work on the Grammar exercise on the middle board. Norma, will you please go back to the cloakroom with Dorothy and Madeline and work on your plans for the Red Cross meeting. You can get the board work done later. Grenville and Tommy, you work on spelling exercise 104 on page 96 of your spellers. Kathleen and Geraldine get out your exercise books and I'll be around to help you with your printing."

At recess, we went outside and played "fox and goose," and just when we had worked up a good sweat, the bell rang and we were back at it. We recited multiplication tables, took our time at squeaking our way through blackboard numbers and read aloud till noon. Then the commander and her troops supplemented their lunches with some tapioca pudding, better known as "frog's eyes," heated on top of the stove.

After lunch we produced our pennies for Norma's Junior Red Cross meeting, then returned to mundane matters of history and geography.

Fourth Book closed my day with memory work, and I still remember my rendition:

> Oft in the stilly night,
> E're slumber's chain has bound me
> Fond memory brings the light
> Of other days around me …

And so the day ended. Madeline got to clean the brushes, and Harvey emptied the pail and basin. Grenville emptied the pencil sharpeners and good old Edith tidied up. Then we bundled up for the trek home for rest and repair. So did our heroine, Miss Card.

Free at Last!

Long before my enslavement in the system of education, worthy authorities had decreed that summers would be free of schooling, presumably to allow its young captives to be able to work the fields. By the time I came along, this law had been in effect for more than half a century, and its usefulness had just about run its course. But habits die hard, and thus it was that "summer holidays" became firmly etched on the calendar of the country. You could feel the delicious moment of freedom creep up on you, sometime about the middle of June. It would tickle your fancy, increase your heartbeat, and warm your skin all over. By the last week you began to fidget in class, and visions of summer delights would dance through your head, knocking all serious thought and bits of knowledge from your brain. On last dismissal, you would rush madly from the school's yard and be halfway home before you stopped for breath. Only when you got home would reality sink in. You were not really free at all. You merely had been transferred back to base camp for the summer. To confirm that fact Mother saw us coming up the lane and called out, "Lloyd! You're just in time! I need you to run over to Mrs. Beathune's house and borrow some baking powder for me. There's a good boy."

Even though we still had our chores to do, there was a sense of freedom about it all, and I enjoyed the luxury of lying on the grass, sorting out in my mind what I wished most to do. Within a few moments I had a list as long as my arm—and not one item included the word "berry."

Activities just sort of presented themselves naturally to us as the summer days went by. One popular instrument of creativity was the jackknife. Every boy had one; and one of the first things we made was the catapult (known farther south as the sling-shot). We would cut the crotch of a small elder, cut two rubber bands from a discarded tire tube, shape a pocket from the tongue of an old shoe, and fasten them all together to make what we fondly called a "caddy." We vied with one another to become the "best shot" in the neighbourhood, as we selected fine round stones from the road and went into the bush searching for game. The odd squirrel fell victim to our savagery, and insulators on telephone lines made tempting targets. Otherwise, it was mostly bravado and a lot of fuss. Bows and arrows were a passing fancy, but they almost always gave way to the "caddy."

We were great whittlers too. A whistle could easily be made from the same elder and pieces of cedar soon became boats, aeroplanes, and spiles. Often, our summer pleasure would be interrupted by the howling of old Jumbo, who would come waddling into the house with his nose full of porcupine quills. This demanded Dad's attention. He would go to work with the pliers while we held the whining dog. It was a nasty business, messing with a porcupine; but their lumbering, clumsy gait, coupled with a benign appearance, repeatedly invited our dog to investigate. The result was always disaster. It sometimes led to more than the pain of removal. Hidden quills often caused infections, which prolonged the painful lesson that Jumbo had been delivered. He learned slowly, however, and later in the summer he would present himself again, pleading for the pliers.

One of our most engaging adventures was provided by the fireflies, which came in early summer. With the coming of twilight, the low-lands would gradually fill with dots of darting light which, to a child, appeared as one of the wonders of the world. We knew little of the scientific explanation for this phenomenon. We only knew that by some magic, these flying glow-worms would arrive in the early summer to tickle our fancy, and send us scampering for the nearest jar. As the season wore on, children throughout the countryside could be seen dashing in and out of the bushes with their jars, ready to capture their prey. "Lightning-bugs" we called them; and it was always a contest see who had the most at the end of the hunt. We would look at them, and marvel at their pulsating glow. We wanted to take them to bed with us, and boast that we could read by their collective light. And some of us would listen with wide eyes when an elder would tell of the time in his youth when, in an isolated bush cabin, a doctor performed an operation solely by the light cast by lightning-bugs crowded into a huge jar! By morning most of us would set our prisoners free to glow again in another evening twilight.

Nature called us to the lake, too. At Martin's Siding it was Siding Lake, a muddy, swamp-bordered body of water that only had its waves to welcome us. (Appropriately, we called it Mud Lake.) Its bottom was a leech-infested layer of mud that defied us to tread upon it. But, adventurous souls that we were, the murky depths served only to dare us—and we accepted the challenge. How well I remember the days when we competed for the honour of having the most bloodsuckers clinging to our legs when we emerged from a dip in the muddy lake. A sprinkle of salt aided in their removal, which led to their being laid on a log and smashed to bits by a blood-thirsty throng of young savages. It was a moment to remember. Skeleton Lake offered us much more inviting swimming. I first explored its eastern end as a little boy where my parents visited and watched while I enjoyed the delights of the beautiful sandy beach, and I grandly rode a drifting log.

I met the other end of the lake when we lived at Ullswater. There, I learned to swim—when my brother threw me in over my head! It was during these years that I first paid the price of ignoring the burning sun, and suffered with the others as the burn ran its course. Eventually, it turned into a manly tan, just in time for school.

One summer experience at Ullswater remains rooted in my mind. They were people from the other side of the tracks, one might say; and I met them through my mother, which only makes sense, considering who we were. They were the tourist people of the early thirties, who had braved the long trip from places like Toronto and Windsor to seek the magic of a Muskoka summer. There they were in their cottages, which stretched along the bay of Skeleton Lake; and there we were, in our modest house that lay up the road from the beach. In real terms, it was less than a mile away. But we were separated by a million miles if one measured by circumstances. Our dad worked at the local mill, and during the summer served as bookkeeper and handyman at the nearby lodge.

Neither of these positions brought us any closer to the tourists, however. No, it was Mother's magic that did the trick. She was a great cook. In fact "Aunt Bessie" was known throughout Muskoka as a master of the dough; and it wasn't long before her reputation seeped down to these cottagers. She was particularly renowned for her Parker House rolls, and, when this notoriety spread to the cottagers, there was no turning back. I can still hear Mrs. Philkins saying, "Mrs Dennis, I have only one complaint about your Parker House rolls. They taste 'more-ish'." It took Mother only a moment to unravel the compliment and accept another order. And by the time the news had spread to Catlin Cottages, Aunt Bessie was in business. The Switzers and the Godwins joined the fray and, before long, Mother's income equalled that of Dad. But times were tough in the early thirties, and my father's English pride, which ordinarily would have difficulty coping with such a breach of custom, was swallowed in silence. When orders for rolls, pies, tea biscuits and jelly-rolls, cookies and crusty bread became a common occurrence, he became a willing agent, and even stooped to deliver the goods, upon occasion.

But regular delivery was largely my job; and although I didn't beg for the position, it became more palatable when Mother suggested that I pick flowers from our garden, and go into business for myself. And that's how I met Phyllis and Irene—and Georgina.

The Catlins were an older couple from the Windsor area. They frequently asked our parents to come to their cottage for an evening of cards. Mrs. Catlin belonged to the Order of the Eastern Star, and Mr. Catlin's brother was a railway engineer who made frequent runs through Muskoka. My parents had belonged to the Lodge in better days, and were no strangers to Muskoka trains, so perhaps they found some common ground. At any rate, they enjoyed one another's company; and more importantly, they had grandchildren who visited them occasionally. Bob was about five years old, Phyllis was nine and Irene was eleven.

So there we were on a summer night on the verandah of the cottage, while our elders played cards in the cottage living room. We were awkward during our first game of "snakes and ladders," but after a few teasing darts from my brother like "Betcha I can spit farther than you," we got down to serious social exploration. Then Irene suggested we play "hospital"—and just as Vernon declared himself a doctor, we were denied "treatment" by the call from our parents that it was time to go.

One day, as I finished my flower sales, I came upon a patch of beauty that I had not seen before. There, before my widening eyes, was a fair-haired girl, playing in a sand-box. She had bare feet, just like me, and as soon as she said hello, I knew that we were kindred spirits.

"What are you doing?" I asked.

"I'm playing house," she answered almost proudly. "Would you like to play?"

"Maybe," I answered tentatively. "Is that your doll?"

"Yes, I call her Ruby." And when I said that I too, had a doll, she never batted an eye.

"What's your doll's name?"

"Mary," I answered.

The truth is that I'd always had a doll. Perhaps it was prompted by my mother's erstwhile desire to have a daughter that prompted her to so equip me. Whatever the reason, it seemed that a doll had lurked in my childhood as long as I could remember. And not until this occasion had I so readily admitted her existence to the outside world.

"Would you like to bring Mary down to visit my Ruby?"

"Sure," I said. "I can come this afternoon if you like."

"Come at two o'clock," answered Georgina.

And that's how Mary got out of the closet. Mother gave me a knitted bag, in which to carry her, which was more for my protection than that of my doll. Armed with such a toy, an accidental meeting with Clyde or Harvey was too horrible to contemplate. I furtively clutched the bag under my arm and hurried off to enjoy a whole new dimension of friendship. It continued throughout the summer, and was even made more eventful by a hike to a nearby falls with a picnic lunch, in company with my mother and Georgina's grandmother.

Sadly, summer came to an end, and so did playing house with Georgina. The Catlins, the Philkins, the Switzers and the Godwins all retreated to their southern fortresses, leaving the rest of us to return to the normal life of Muskoka. I hung up the knitted bag, and put Mary back in the closet. Perhaps next year.

Between our flights to bush and lake, our usual chores somehow got done; but they were well down the list of things to conquer. Nature came first. And we could see the end coming. It began with the turning of the odd leaf on the trees in the bush, and the storage of hay and oats in the barn and sheds. A trip to town resulted in new equipment for school like scribblers, pen and ink. An eraser came along for the ride. The berry pail cleaned up its act and offered itself as a container for my school lunch. A new cotton shirt showed up with a pair of shorts, which had already seen service with my brother.

And for the first day of school in the fall, I wore shoes on condition that I could then go barefoot till the first sign of frost. Mother agreed, knowing full well that her partner, Mother Nature, would drive me into shoes long before that. And she did. In two weeks, I was properly shod, and ready for whatever the fates of Fall had to offer. One thing was certain: the freedom of summer died with the lightning-bugs, and we were back in jail till next year.

The Fall Fair

One of the colourful pieces of patchwork that first displayed the life and times of Canada was the fall fair.

From coast to coast, nearly every community was bonded once a year by the compelling attraction of this event; and rare indeed is the Canadian with rural roots who cannot boast of having attended one at least once during his childhood.

Most of them were not grand affairs. Indeed, most were quite modest and offered little by way of urban attraction. Nevertheless, they provided refreshing interest for grown-ups, and heart-pounding excitement for the young.

Long before the actual event, the fair reached out to capture the imagination of young and old alike; and teachers, farmers and housewives began planning and preparing their handiwork for the show of the year.

The casual observer, of course, had little idea of the time and trouble involved in such preparations. Months before the actual event, the competitive urge would rise in the rural households, and everything from the syrup borne at the end of March to the pies baked on the day before judgement took their turns for attracting the care and attention of the entrant.

Vegetables, still in the ground, were diligently cared for, and young calves just born were carefully groomed for the great event. Russell Mawhinney polished the harnesses of his renowned team of Clydesdales and prepared once more to win the weight-pull. Sheep were clipped and cleaned, hens were fattened, and jars were filled with jams and jellies, all with an eye on the red ribbon that said to the world, "First Prize."

Teachers at the schools surrounding the fair's location were just as busy. There were essays to write, pictures to paint and handwriting to be done—and done again. Boys built birdhouses and girls stitched samplers. And all of them practised, over and over again, the physical exercises and the school yell.

"Arms side! Arms in! Arms up! Arms down! Arms out! Arms down! Arms back! Arms front! Arms down!" commanded the teacher, over and over. Each school endlessly practised the prescribed exercises in the vain hope that, on the appointed day, the judge would find something extra special in this performance.

In 1934, our teacher at S.S. #2 Watt in Ullswater was "something special." For a month before the Utterson Fall Fair, she had us practise these monotonous exercises with all the authority of a drill sergeant. But she did something else, too. She wrote a school yell which was guaranteed to raise the spirits of Ullswater, if not the folks at the Fair in Utterson. How well I remember the sixteen of us standing like a children's choir, and belting out with all our might, "Caninny, cananny, cananny canoo! With a hullaba, hullaba, hullaballo! Rickety, rackety, rackety roo! U-L-L-S-W-A-T-E-R! That's how you spell it! This is how you yell it! Ullswater! Ullswater! Rah! Rah! Rah!"

This would be followed by our sweeter rendering of "The Maple Leaf Forever" and "God Save the King."

Let those kids from Beatrice, Port Sydney, Raymond, Bent River—and even Utterson, itself—take us on! We'll show 'em all!

We had other things to show off, too. Many of us grew our own vegetables and flowers for show, and some of the boys built birdhouses and whittled objects from pine. Plasticine was another popular medium of the day, and I well remember a snake which I moulded, ready for the great event.

Today, the Utterson Fair is only a memory. Its parade and show grounds are overgrown and neglected, and its hall put to other uses. But in the thirties, it was alive and well, and attracted people for miles around.

Pigs and cows, cocks and hens and sleek, freshly-groomed horses vied with calves and sheep for public attention.

A hawker or two would call out the beauty of his wares, and several children like myself would beg to become the owner of a propeller on a stick, or a ball of cotton candy.

Ice cream was there, too; but, as I recall, only one treat was allowed. Cotton candy and ice cream make you sick, according to my mother. And I didn't want to get sick. I had to be ready to do my bit with the school yell which we were to perform at noon.

Meanwhile, a steady stream of people threaded through the hall, admiring all the treasures of baking, sewing, knitting, scholastic endeavours and assorted handicrafts. My plasticine snake was there, along with my brother's birdhouse. Rich and fancy, poor and simple, they all waited for the judgement that would render them famous or forgotten.

At noon, it seemed that all the world had gathered to see us strut our stuff. When S.S.#2 Watt marched proudly onto the parade ground with our banner fluttering at the front, we just knew that we were the best. And when we bellowed out "Caninny, cananny," we just knew that the prize was ours.

My big test was near at hand. It came in the form of a spelling match, in which the champions of each school were pitted against one another. I was proud to represent Ullswater, and was sure that I could win over my cousin Sethie who had been chosen to represent Utterson.

Privately, it was a matter of some moment for me. Sethie lived "in town," had a bicycle and even an indoor toilet. I felt that I could even the score by putting him down.

One by one, the school inspector called out words, and one by one the adversaries fell, finding themselves no match for "hepatica," "nasturtium" or even "alluvial."

Finally there were only two contestants left—Sethie and I.

"Lloyd Dennis!" boomed the inspector, "Spell 'cauliflower'!"

Suddenly feeling very much in the spotlight, I began with great trepidation, "c-a-u-l-i-f-l ..." I paused. Just how did the danged word finish? I could feel the eyes of my mother and Aunt Lizzie bearing down upon me—to say nothing of my classmates, for whom I must do—or die. "... o-u-r," I finished.

"Out!" boomed the inspector. "Sethie Grimes, spell 'cauliflower'!"

Sethie drew himself up to his full four feet and fairly shouted, "Cauliflower. C-a-u-l-i-f-l-o-w-e-r."

"Utterson is declared the winner of the spelling match," announced the inspector. The crowd clapped, and Sethie strutted over to his mother, Aunt Lizzie.

For the next forty years, I couldn't bear the idea of eating that vegetable whose name led me to such a humiliating defeat.

There was one saving grace. I won the third highest number of points that year, and received a book for my efforts. It was *The Rock and the River* by Ralph Connor, provided by the T. Eaton Company. Another was won by my brother in 1931 for winning second highest number of points. It was called *Wacousta*, and told the story of the Pontiac Conspiracy, a choice bit of early Canadian history.

These books are all that remain of my adventures at the Utterson Fair. Why, even the donors are gone.

But that cauliflower is still here. Indeed, I'm having it for dinner tonight!

Wheels of Fortune

It was just a discarded tire from an old car; but, fuelled with my imagination, it became a chariot of fire that could lift me above the dusty road of Martin's Siding and carry me grandly along to the castle of my dreams. Being only six years old, I was allowed such fantasies. Indeed, they were expected of me, and I gave them full rein. In my bare feet, I would slap the tire along the road that ran before our house, and try my best to get the tire to throw dust, just as Dad's car did. Dust was a great motivator. The more my tire could spew up, the greater the power of its magic; and, aside from the odd confrontation with hen manure, which would momentarily foul my manual motor, such runs along the road were worth the effort. I had taken the first step in my love affair with the wheel.

A brief romance with an old tricycle ended on Brown's hill when Mr. Armstrong backed down the hill and accidentally ran over my back wheels. My head swelled with pride. Barely seven years old, and I was already a veteran with one accident to my credit! With the tricycle beyond repair, I went back to my tire and rode the dust again.

When we moved to Ullswater in 1930, I found new mobility. It was a light wheelbarrow, which, seen by ordinary eyes, was a tool of toil. But for a youngster bereft of wheels, it easily became a vehicle of class. Round and round the yard I would run with my new love, making all the appropriate noises to give it the power that such a machine required. Of course I knew about bicycles by this time, and saw them regularly in Eaton's catalogue. But I knew better than to ask for one. They were too costly, even for Santa Claus. I contented myself with the wheelbarrow, and would even deign to carry wood or vegetables in it from time to time. But loaded or empty, it was a tool of pleasure.

A new wheel forced itself upon me by the time I was ten. Orland Olsen's father was the village blacksmith, and he provided the source of my next wheel of fortune. It was the hoop, the iron ring that held the hub of wagon wheels of the time. With a little practice, I could push that hoop along with the best of them. A crossed bar on the end of a stick would be cut with notches and one could "shift gears" as he ran, just by moving the bar to the right or left. We all had hoops, and used them as vehicles to go to and from school. New models were developed, using spools instead of bars. "Cuts down the friction," Orland declared. "Makes goin' to school a lot easier."

He was right; and the ordinary hoop became almost air-worthy when we added a spool halfway up the shaft. With a cardboard propeller fastened to it, and a pulley of string running to the lower spool, we fairly flew to school. I felt like Billy Bishop on these runs, and dreamed of the day when my hoop would carry me above the earth and into the sky—perhaps to become a hero just like him.

Dad, too, had a yearning for wheels; Grandma had brought her horse Jessie, complete with buggy and cutter, when she came to live with us. Still they didn't have the status offered by the automobile.

However, he had married well. My mother's brother, Seth, was one of Muskoka's earliest automobile entrepreneurs, and had opened a garage in Allensville. In no time at all, Alf Dennis found himself the proud owner of a succession of used cars that changed our lives. A 1926 Star took the family to Flint, Michigan, to visit my grandfather, while I stayed forlornly at the Darlings' home. A 1930 Model "A" Ford took us to Huntsville to sell the turkeys in 1932. And it had enough life in it to take us to the Canadian National Exhibition in 1933.

In the thirties, a trip to Toronto was a far cry from what it is today. The car had to be cranked to get it started, lacked a heater for warmth, and almost guaranteed frequent stops because of tire failure. Such an occasion usually required not only the removal of the wheel, but tube repair right on the spot. This test of nerves and skill was not an isolated event; in fact a repair job might be expected several times during one trip. I seem to remember three such stops on our trip to the Exhibition. But at least it wasn't winter!

A Whippet came and went in the night, and a durable old Durant was with us when we lost the house at Ullswater and were scattered like leaves in the wind. While Dad and my brother headed north for work, the Durant stood a lonely vigil in the yard where Mother and I waited in Utterson. Perhaps the poor old thing remembered more glorious days when Dad would let Vernon and me ride the front fenders as we rode off gloriously from Ullswater to Huntsville.

Then there was that unfortunate incident in 1936 when my brother Vernon forsook his family in the logging camp and returned to Huntsville with the urge to bring Dad's old car back to life and run up a fuel bill while he cruised the streets of the town. Dad's chariot at that time was a 1934 Dodge.

My great moment came in 1937, when I received my beautiful C.C.M. bicycle from my poor but generous parents. I felt like Buck Rogers as I flew along the streets and roads of Huntsville, and only returned to earth two months later when I came out of school one day to find it stolen. Fortune seemed so fleeting in those days.

But it didn't forsake me entirely. I got a job after school that fall, and before long I was mobile again—and this time I had bought the steed myself. It was a red Glider, which I convinced myself was every bit as good as my stolen C.C.M.

As for Dad, he became a veteran owner of used cars, courtesy of Uncle Seth. By the time I left school, he had consumed at least four more tired chariots, "as is," guaranteed to last for miles and miles. As for Seth, his fortune grew as he moved from one location to another. A well-known Chrysler dealer, he even had the honour of displaying the car used by the Royal Couple during part of their tour in 1939. Talk about class! Why, just the thought of it made my English-born father stand taller!

I grew taller too. I quit school at sixteen and went to work at the munitions plant in Nobel. The following year, when a young doctor joined the army, I bought his car. It was a 1932 Pontiac coupé, complete with a rumble seat—a true chariot of fire. As I took it for a test run, I was too excited to appreciate that I had moved from a rubber tire to a whole car in just ten years. Talk about wheels of fortune!

The Magical Music of Winter

I could hear it coming, as the leaves fell in the Fall. Flocks of Canada geese honked their way on training flights in preparation for the trip south. I could see it too, as Mother reviewed her inventory of long underwear, mitts, scarves and socks. And if that weren't enough to warn us, her admonition was: "You hear that winter wind a-howlin' boys, so you know what's comin'! Winter's on the way, and there'll be no time for foolin' around while that wood-box's standin' empty. Land's sakes! You'd think there was a train comin'! Listen to the whine and whistle of that wind. Why it's even flapping the shingles on the shed!"

There were many notes offered by the music of Winter's symphony. As I lie awake at night, I wonder at them, even now. And I'm struck by the realization that although it was Winter's music, most members of the community played the instruments. Thinking about it, I feel privileged to be among the minority of the world's people who have played in such an orchestra—which restricts its tours to cold climates.

Of course, that howling wind was only the overture. To get to the main body of the piece, one had to wait for the first fall of snow. That's when I was allowed to join the music makers. I would step outside on a snow-covered frosty morning and listen to the creaky crunch made by my rubbers upon the frozen path. As I walked, I seemed to grow more powerful, somehow, as if the two rubbers were motorized to crunch, creak, crunch, creak their way up the path and along the road to school. What other sound could match those cold, dry, brittle notes that emerged with every step! And, on very cold days, the wires strung along the road gave forth a mysterious background hum to complement the crunch of my rubbers on the snow.

Other sounds joined the symphony of winter. Even now, I close my eyes and listen as men wielding a cross-cut saw execute a group of trees in the bush. Suddenly, a loud crack is heard. A call rings through the forest. "Timber!" And with an agonizing ripping sound, the once-tall tree comes crashing to the ground, taking several of its yelping young with it. After 200 years, it is no more.

A team of horses emerges from the bush, pulling a load of logs. As if to vie with my rubbers for uniqueness of sound, the sleigh's runners emit a curious squeak as they slide across the snow. Unlike my rubbers, they play a score of notes, and their squeals rise and fall according to the varying ease of their glide upon the road. It might be a stretch to add the team to the orchestra, but I can hear the squeak of the harness, the blubbering snorts of the horses, and even the breaking of wind that somehow seems harmonious with the surrounding sounds of winter.

Later, in the freezing night, the remaining trees of the bush, as if in requiem to the fallen, periodically snap—and our house joins in with a resounding crack. Our teacher said that these are the sounds of wood contracting in the cold. But I knew better. It was the sound of sadness and loss in the forest.

Then, the nearby lake would give voice with a boom that could be heard for miles. Was it joining the trees in their lamentation? Or was it suffering a loss of its own? Earlier that week someone had cut into it and removed huge chunks to store in the ice house that stood on the shore. As the saw slipped back and forth to make the cut, its sound was not that of cutting wood. It was—well, you would have to hear it to really appreciate its dry zip, zop, zip. A winter sound to be sure. To add variation, the big chunks sounded like slithering glass as they were hauled aboard the waiting sleigh for their one and only ride to the ice house.

On a very cold winter night one might expect that the orchestra would rest. But it didn't. Of course the trees snapped and the ice boomed, but there was more. People far away could suddenly be heard. A distant dog would bark, and somewhere in the dark, a pack of wolves would howl in tune. And, on a really cold night, the whistle of a far-off train would lead my imagination to another world. Only the freezing voice of Winter could work such magical music. And to top it off the whole of Mother Nature often flung a banner of beauty into the sky. The dictionary called the banner the Aurora Borealis. We knew it as the northern lights, and there were those among us who swore that we could actually hear those shifting silvery shafts of light. For the unbeliever, there was always the staccato beat of the pileated woodpecker, as he knocked on wood behind the barn. He, of course, belonged to the percussion section!

Shovelling snow offered a variety of sounds. Hard-packed deep snow required an effort much like cutting a giant cake, while clearing light fluffy flakes produced notes like feathers being brushed aside. And when you got down to the hard-pan of the path, scraping it gave you the scuttling sound of a job well done.

A ride in the cutter behind our horse Jessie had its own sweet sound. The squeak of the cutters' runners was softer than that of the sleighs, high pitched and airy. As if to add weight to their effort, Jessie regularly threw clods of snow from her hooves against the cutter's dashboard. And, lest she be out-done by the log team, she contributed some wind of her own—from both ends of her body.

With our skis we added more notes to the music of winter. On a fine, crisp day, we would slip along the crust with strides similar to those used with our skates on ice. But when the weather worsened, we would plop along, breaking trail in the deep snow. And, should Winter's opus hit a warm day, the snow spoke with a guttural sound, and threatened to clog our steeds if we had failed to wax them well enough.

No winter symphony would be complete without its bells. Beautiful at any time, the bells of winter had a special ring. For every teamster, the bells of his horses were a source of pride, a sound that lifted the heart on a heavy day.

Jessie had bells too—and so did the shafts of her cutter. Even our dog, Jumbo, had bells on his harness. He is long gone; but I still get comfort from shaking his harness from time to time, remembering the days when he made music in Muskoka.

On a clear day, the teacher's bell could be heard for miles, and the bell of the community church seemed more melodious when rung for Old Man Winter. Even the odd dog and cat would join the parade, ringing the bells on their collars in tune with all the others.

There were other sounds close to a boy's heart that were heard only in winter. One was the slapping sound created when a home-made hockey stick connected with a frozen lump of horse manure.

Later, this tribal beat would be refined by real skates, a rubber puck and a stick from Eaton's. All three planted a national tune deep in the Canadian psyche. And to add a flourish to the sound, Foster Hewitt would watch as Hockey Night in Canada passed by, and call out "He shoots! He scores!" Although the tune played only in season, its notes would reverberate long after the music of Winter died away.

The ice section of Winter's musicians was not confined to the lakes. When it covered the road, Dad took up his instrument and added more tortured notes. He would fix chains to the car's rear wheels and off we would go, clattering away to town. New notes were usually added, unwanted, but inevitable. A link would break in one of the chains, causing it to strike the fender with every turn of the wheel. Sometimes Dad had wire handy to fasten the unruly one. But as often as not, we would go clattering home, with the discordant member of the chain gang slap, slap, slapping against the fender. It was a note of discord that the symphony frequently had to suffer—along with Dad!

Icy instruments were there throughout the winter, from beginning to end. Even before the snow arrived, those drips on the eaves suddenly changed to icicles, which grew as winter progressed. Periodically, they would melt, and just as one got used to their drip, drip, drip, they would suddenly grow silent, and longer. Then one would go crashing down, startling everyone who happened to be nearby.

When the ice put on a show, it was awesome and silent. It would cover all and sundry with a glistening blanket that shivered and shimmered for only a moment. Then it would add its music to Winter as it dropped tinkling to the ground below. Such shows were brief but beautiful, and never failed to attract the attention of the audience.

And those icicles? They opened the opus, and they were also at the end. Bit by bit, as the waters of the creeks gushed forth, those needles of ice grew shorter and shorter. And when the last one fell, the adults warned their young that the ice on the lake was thin. Awesome stories were told of those who had failed to notice that Old Man Winter was about to retire for another year.

But not yet. Just as we were about to get out of that long underwear and put our mitts away, a blue-jay called to announce a final blast from the trumpets of Mother Nature. It reminded us all not to "get too cocky," as Mother put it. The wind would howl around the eaves, and the ground that was bare the night before had a new coat in the morning, as pure as the driven snow—which, of course, is what it was. But it was only a parting shot. We laughed it off, and prepared to join the band called "Spring."

It All Comes Out in the Wash

My mother was an up-to-date woman of the bush. Not for her the endless, back-breaking toil of scrubbing clothes on a flat rock beside some wayward stream. No sir! She had the best basic equipment that could be found in Eaton's catalogue: two washtubs hung on the wall of the porch, beside a gleaming washboard. On the floor stood a copper boiler, and on the shelf above sat a box of blueing. And clothespins? Dozens of them lay crowded in an old flour bag, eager to get into the battle that began each Monday morning. Empty but equally eager, two galvanized pails stood ready to answer the call to duty. And mother had additional weaponry outside. There was a post with clothesline and pole, and wood for the cookstove, all supplied by the nearby bush. A mountain of snow lay just outside the door ready to provide water for boiling. And should she prefer to use the well, it lay only forty yards away, complete with well-hook. All that apparatus needed was a young slave—and there I was.

I exaggerate of course. Getting the water and the wood was a rudimentary but simple task. The great feat lay in turning that dirty inventory of cloth and clothing into pristine piles of purity, come rain or snow, come hell or high water. By Sunday night, the armour and ammunition lay ready and waiting for the great attack, which would begin right after breakfast. I can tell you, hell hath no fury like a mother thwarted on the day of the wash. One's life wouldn't be worth a tinker's damn if those pails weren't as full as the woodbox. And a boy that failed to produce his quota of dirty socks and underwear—well he might be better to run to school and stay there. But if he did come home at the end of the day, he would see that his mother had won another battle in the War of the Washing. He had only to look at the trophies fluttering and flapping in the breeze, held up before the eyes of the world by the faithful clothesline and the stalwart clothes-pole. Like most boys, he would give scant attention to this evidence of hard work. He was used to it. It happened every Monday, year in and year out. Wasn't that what all mothers did on Mondays?

Mother customarily opened the engagement on Sunday night, when she sorted the wash and put some of it to soak; and only she could appreciate what a range of articles the family offered up for attention. They ranged from overalls to bloomers, from her own stockings to the rough, hand-knit socks of her men-folk. In winter the list would include long underwear, sweaters, heavy shirts, toques and mitts. Then there were the sheets, flannel blankets and pillowcases, the odd hooked rug, towels, curtains, runners and assorted cloth that had seen earlier service as flour and sugar bags. And it was not just the quantity of items that presented themselves for attention. It was the variety. Some items, why even I could have washed them. But others required great skill and judgement in handling, lest they shrink, fade, stretch, run or even disappear in the process. But Bessie Dennis was equal to the task. After all, she had been washing every Monday long before I came upon the scene, and seemed to know what she was doing.

She sorted and soaked, and boiled in the copper boiler. She scrubbed in one tub and rinsed in the other, adding blueing to sharpen the whites. Then she hung it all to dry. As we would say today, "it was no big deal."

But it was a big deal. Just bringing that water to a boil on the stove was a chore in itself. And scrubbing! Only those who have tried it know the agony of a thousand rubs with the same finger-tips—with fully 100 of them with no cloth between the fingers and the ribs of the board! Dad had made a wash bench for Mother; but still she had to bend over the tub. And it's little wonder that she would straighten periodically, arch her back, and wipe the sweat from her brown. Then it was back to the board again, to scrub and probably curse the writer of "The Irish Washerwoman," a dance tune popular at the time. I can hear her thinking, "I betcha it was a man that wrote that!"

Washing the different loads was bad enough. But have you ever had to wring out a flannel blanket—by yourself? Mind you, the blankets didn't appear in every wash. But when they did, they demanded equal treatment, and it was all Mother could do to hold one end under the arm and twist the other till it looked like an elephant's trunk. Then back and over, and do it again. The sheets were almost as bad; besides, there were more of them, and they presented themselves more frequently. Add a touch of arthritis or an aching joint or two, and you had the ingredients of surrender or retreat. But Mother did neither. When we came home from school, those blankets and sheets would be hanging out there with the other stuff, mute evidence of my mother's will to win.

There were other tasks that required more skill than brawn. Having the right soap was one of them. As I recall, Mother preferred Comfort or Sunlight, in yellow bars. More importantly, she had to know just how to add the blueing to her white articles, so that it wouldn't cake or stain. She used it in a little sack, as I remember. Drying Dad's socks was another test. Lest they shrink while drying, she would put them on wire stretchers, and hang them behind the stove.

Starching was another skill that demanded care. Mind you, she didn't have many fine items to starch. But, upon occasion, one of Dad's white shirts would leap out and produce its collar and cuffs for special treatment. A bowl with a little starch dissolved in water would appear as if by magic, and just the right amount would be applied before the shirt was dismissed to the clothesline.

On good days, Mother would often get two lines of washing completed by the end of the day. She would arm herself with clothespins, lug out her sodden victims and begin the ritual of putting them out to dry. As the line became loaded, it would begin to sag. Finally, when the line had reached its limit, Mother would go to the centre and raise the pole. With its crotched top snugly in place, she would stand it firmly under the line; then step back, hands on hips, and briefly survey her handiwork. Then it was back to the house to clean up. With any luck and a good wind, she could have that line in by noon and another out and dry before supper.

A little luck and a good wind. That's what everyone in Mother's position would ask for. But that was not always available; and bad luck often showed up on wash days. Imagine the storm that blew up just as the line was dry, when all the scurrying in the world couldn't save the wash from drowning. Then there was the day the wind was so strong that it snapped the pole and allowed the sheets to reach for safety on the grass below. And what about that good sock of Lloyd's? Mother swore that two went on the line, but only one survived. She even had her son search the yard after school, but it was nowhere to be found.

The worst of the Washing War was in the winter. At twenty, even thirty degrees below zero, Mother would go out bravely, and with bare fingers pin her treasures to the line. There was no turning back, no time out. In war and in washing it was over the top and charge ahead. Like the good soldier that she was, Mother carried on, often against great odds, while I came home complaining of the cold, scarcely glancing at the washing on the line.

One winter afternoon I came home from school just after Mother had taken in the wash. There, like ghostly visitors, stood our long underwear against the wall. As I had no playmates nearby, I was sorely tempted to play with the long johns. But gradually they melted away to become nothing more than limp piles of long underwear.

You might assume that, with the gathering in of the wash, the war was over. But now a new battle presented itself. This time, the weapons were ready and waiting on the stove. A group of flatirons, their black sides gleaming ominously, seemed almost eager to join the fray. Above them, on top of the warming closet, sat their means of travel. It was the handle. And when all was ready Mother would grasp it, zoom down and allow its claw to clamp onto the waiting iron. Thus equipped, she was ready for the final battle.

In the War of the Wash, some women preferred the first battle to the last; and Mother was one of those. She was undoubtedly good in skirmishes with the iron; but she was a robust woman, and much preferred the knock-down, drag-'em-out tousles in the suds and soap to the gentle patience required by the iron. But both were part of the same chore, really, and she gave the iron and the wash-board equal attention.

She didn't have an ironing-board. Instead, she used the flat surface of the kitchen table, covered by several layers of flannelette sheet. She dutifully faced the pile of clean but wrinkled laundry and, picking up the iron she touched it with her wet finger to test its readiness. If it was hot enough, she was off to the races—figuratively speaking, of course!

Finally, in the soft glow of the lamp, the Dennis Washing stood in neat rows, waiting to be made dirty again. Dad's white shirt lay apart from the rest. After all, it was no ordinary article of the house. And neither was my Mother. And whether it was soiled laundry or sinning souls, she had one redeeming saying: "It all comes out in the wash."

Where's the Eaton's Catalogue?

It was a common question in those days. The Dennis family was like most rural families across Canada. It gave Eaton's catalogue a position well "above the salt" when it came to household necessities and even our dog Jumbo afforded it at least a passing glance.

For Mother, its arrival in the mail opened the door of dreams. With unabashed excitement, she would sit at the table and flick through its pages of endless invitation, from bloomers to blouses, from corsets to cotton dresses, and on to coats and curtains. Hats? Every type imaginable displayed itself, hoping to catch her eye. And if her inclinations were more practical, a long parade of housewares, from soap to sideboards, marched by page after page, until she was forced to say to Dad, "I swear, Alf, I can't think of a single thing that a family could need that isn't in this catalogue! Look! There is a page of real wallpaper! All we'd have to do to paper that wall in the parlour is mark the number of rolls we'd need, and send it in to Eaton's. They'll send it to us by mail."

"That's right," said Dad. "That's why it's called a mail-order catalogue. Here's a better idea: collect that page from all your friends and you don't have to order." It was Dad's idea of Depression humour.

Of course, it wasn't long before he had his nose stuck in the catalogue too; for it offered an equal array of items to attract male interest. It offered Dad a two-piece, all-wool suit for less than $20, and a pair of trousers for only $2. Since he was a skilled carpenter, his eyes sought out the saws, where, on page 338, one jumped out at him for only $1.50.

And on pages 342 and 343, more than 200 household items splashed out in a wide display, from door-knobs at two for five cents, to paring knives for five cents each. A good cook stove could be ours for $30, and if a fence were needed, we could order about sixteen feet for another $30. Page 354 offered a complete harness for our horse Jessie for only $17.

I took my turn "window shopping" in the catalogue—after my brother, of course. There was a good jersey for only 43 cents and braces for half as much. There was a cap I liked for $1, but, to tell the truth, none of the clothing items caught my eye as much as the toys. There, to my great delight, was a real wind-up train on its own tracks, for only $1.35! And just on the next page was a tricycle for $12.95 and a peddle-car for $9.75. A real Fleet-Wing wagon, at $6, was beyond my reach. But there were lots of other toys to drool over. I saw a doll carriage that I imagined my friend Norma Creasor would like. But it probably was beyond her, too. It cost almost $10!

It was an amazing thing, the Eaton's catalogue. About ten by twelve inches in size, its Fall and Winter edition contained almost 800 pages. Many of the articles displayed were coloured, all were clearly, even enticingly described, and offered at prices that seemed unbeatable. And, just in case the family wore it out by finger shopping, a Spring and Summer edition would arrive about six months after its older brother. It burst into the Spring like a flower in the mail; and Mother, whenever she could spare a moment, began to thumb anew. This time the display was more geared to summer needs, and artfully offered new styles wherever possible. Like its predecessor, it came complete with ordering instructions and shipping procedures. It offered only about 400 pages, but it was still sufficient to delight the shopping senses.

I found the Fall and Winter edition more to my liking, perhaps because it arrived as the nights grew longer, and was a welcome addition to the lamp-lit table. It was thumbed through, flipped and pawed over until it began to take on the appearance of an old cushion. Items were underlined, framed, crossed out and cut out, and the Dennis family dog-eared so many pages that one half expected it to bark.

Over at Norma's house, the Creasor catalogue underwent additional attack. She, like girls across the country, cut out figures and dresses, and created a family of dolls—each with its own wardrobe! I saw them at school once. The dresses were cut with little tabs that could be folded around the doll figures; and the variety of paper people offered by the catalogue was limited only by the player's imagination.

Some of my friends used the catalogue as a press. They would go through the annual ritual of gathering Autumn leaves, and lay them out page after page in the catalogue, which would then find itself smothered under some handy weight, such as a block of wood. But the imprisonment was only temporary. The catalogue had grander uses; and soon it would be back in the living-room, being fondled like a family pet—which in a way, is what it was.

By now, the reader probably has recalled other uses that this home companion served. One that I recall was its role as a reader. I didn't sit down and consciously "read" it as a lesson; but when I saw that Arrow Cycle, I wasn't long figuring out that it was "chain drive," had fourteen-inch rubber-tired wheels, and came, complete with horn, for only $12.95. Doubtless, over at her house, Norma had found that doll on the same page and read that it was a "walking, talking doll. Put her over your shoulder and she distinctly says 'Mama.' Hold her by the hands and she will walk with you. Price $1.98." Without realizing it Norma was reading beyond her years—and all thanks to the Eaton's catalogue!

Eaton's catalogue found its way into the classroom in more devious ways. On the eve of Christmas, it was not unusual to see its precious pages cut into strips, fastened into loops and joined to make chains to be draped around the tree. Since it had served its purpose by Fall, the

Spring and Summer edition was available for this service—which was appropriate since it had more coloured pages than its mate.

My grandmother found her own use for the 1933 Spring and Summer edition. After it had completed its normal service, she took it to the table and folded each page from the upper right corner to the middle. Some 400 folds later she ended up with a paper cone that, when fastened back to back, stood a foot high on the table. With a ball of yarn pasted on top and a spray of sparkles on the sides, it stood on the table for all to see. Then, placing it on the floor, Granny proudly introduced it to the world: "Meet my new doorstop."

Of course, the Eaton's catalogue had already established itself firmly in the Canadian psyche long before I arrived on the scene. Had my father been more talkative, he could have enlightened me about its advent in Canadian history. He could have told me that when he arrived as a young immigrant to western Canada in 1902, he and his family found it already there, offering its service. Born in 1884, Eaton's catalogue was already well on its way to fulfilling it's creator's dream—to be the "Homesteader's Bible." In hundreds of thousands of Canadian homes, the catalogue was greeted as a privileged agent, and Mr. Eaton had the great satisfaction of "taking his store" to the rural women, knowing that those in the city were beyond their reach.

In 1903 it took its place in Canadian history when the "Barr Colonists" arrived in the West. In a village of tents where Saskatoon now stands, the unscrupulous Reverend Barr was busy swindling the colonists by selling them provisions at highly inflated prices, when suddenly the catalogue appeared upon the scene. Its attractive prices revealed the truth to them, and hugging them to their breasts, they turned their wrath on their leader. Although he subsequently led them to settle in Lloydminster, they spurned his wares in favour of Mr. Eaton's catalogue. This simple act made a major imprint upon Canadian marketing history. As if to prove the point, at least one Saskatchewan community marked its influence by naming their village "Eatonia."

By that time the catalogue was a household word across the land. It appeared, as needed, in both official languages and, upon occasion, it was requested for use as a reader. Stories abounded about the faith prompted by its presence, as was revealed in a letter to Eaton's asking "if the girl in the red dress on page 30 would be interested in marriage."

Its fame even spread across the seas, where it was viewed with awe by prospective emigrants to Canada. And some still swear Queen Mary used it occasionally to develop the reading skills of her granddaughters, Elizabeth and Margaret.

When the catalogue entered my life, of course, I was not interested in its climb to fame. I was busy using it as a "wonder book." And as the catalogue neared the end of its household service, I looked forward to its transfer to its final resting place, where I could study it more privately. And where was that, you ask? Why, out in the little house, the privy, the back-house, or by whatever name you knew the outdoor toilet. There it sat, on the throne, ready and waiting to perform its last service.

There it was that I really developed my reading skills: "Girls' rayon panties of light meshed rayon for cool summer wear. 2 for 50 cents." Like all boys I yearned to learn about the unknown secrets of life, and found these pages very revealing. I gradually graduated to the girdle pages, and learned that a lattice-back corset could be had for less than $5. I learned a lot about women from the Eaton's catalogue. I suppose you could say it was an early form of family life education. I think that my brother took the same course.

I'm not sure, but I think that Dad was more interested in the tools and harness department. As for my friend Norma, I don't know whether she learned anything from boys' underwear on page 156. It's not likely, since she had brothers. What I do know is that as the winter days passed, this dear old family companion was stripped of its glorious beauty until, by the coming of April, all that was left were a few pages of women's underwear—and the harness section. But the memory of it still lingers on.

Postscript—The ghost of Eaton's catalogue returned just the other day during my reading of a book about of the prisoner-of-war camp in Gravenhurst during the Second World War. The ever ready catalogue was delivered to the prisoners regularly. They took advantage of its offer and grew accustomed to ordering towels and other necessities that they could afford. Talk about service!

Lamplighting Time

I can hear that old song still, pouring out of the gramophone as though it were yesterday. It had become very popular early in the Depression, and announced itself to me by way of Tex Ritter, a country singer of that period. I was never to learn the details of the song's lament; but I was familiar with the lamp to which it refers. It, and other members of the lamp family, were constant companions during the years of my childhood. Here is Tex Ritter, with "When It's Lamplighting Time in the Valley":

> There's a lamp shining bright in the window,
> In the window it's shining for me
> And I know that my mother is waiting
> For a boy she is pining to see.
> *Refrain:*
> When its lamplighting time in the valley
> Then in dreams I go back to my home;
> I can see that old lamp in the window,
> It will guide me wherever I roam.
>
> In the lamplight each night I can see her,
> As she rocks in her chair to and fro;

And she prays that I'll come back to see her,
Yet I know that I never can go.

So she lights up the lamp and sits waiting
For she knows not the crime I have done;
So I'll change all my ways and I'll meet her,
Up in Heaven, when life's race is won.

Like many children of the time, I lived without benefit of electricity. But, as Mother said, "you don't miss what you never had," so I scarcely noticed the inconvenience. Mind you, it did present certain slave labour that I disliked intensely. One task that I found particularly forbidding was cleaning the lamps. A sooty lamp and a ten-year-old boy had very little in common in those days, a fact that my mother failed to appreciate. Thus, she fell into the habit of assigning the job to me.

The lamp itself was no problem. A simple globe of glass on a pedestal was satisfied with a good wipe. Even the brass head and wick were friendly enough. A little polish satisfied one, and a trim with scissors met the needs of the other. But the chimney was another matter. Most of its dirt lay on the inside, and involved the crumpling of old newspapers and reaching ever so carefully inside to wipe the thing clean. It was not as simple as it sounded, because the glass was fragile, and provided an open invitation to disaster. A breakage was bad enough; but if it happened to explode when there was no spare in the house ... well, the consequence was one reason why I hated the job.

But there's no denying the fact that the simple lamp, shining into the darkness of a winter night, offered a warm beacon of comfort to whoever might approach it. It was more than a light, somehow. It was a haven of safety and fellowship, even of love. And there are many who, notwithstanding the relatively more primitive life-style of which the lamp was a part, will recall its light with a sense of nostalgic longing for the times which it embraced. Oft-times it ruled supreme, as the sole source of light in the home, and all living creatures caught within its rays were subject to its magic. Mother embraced it as she prepared dinner in the gathering dark. It lit our supper table, and brought light—if not enlightenment—to our evening sessions of homework and reading. When we went to bed, we didn't turn it off. We blew it out. If there were another upstairs, it was lit in turn; if not, Old Faithful was carried up to the bedroom by Mother. Then darkness reigned; not the darkness of today, but the utter darkness of a house in the country without light.

Wending our way home from school on a winter day, it was the lamp in the window that drew us along that last mile. One would think that it was possessed of a magic power, so strong was its pull. It was only a flickering flame of a wick soaked in oil; but, in the mind of the approaching youth, it spoke of warmth, food, safety—and rescue from the cruelty of the real world. I can see it yet.

That lamp had a brother. He was the coal-oil lantern, and he did most of his work beyond the lamp's domain. He, too, was a simple contraption consisting chiefly of a squat, round metal tank supporting a globe encased in a wire bracket. This was topped by a metal shade from which a wire handle reached up to whoever should choose to carry it.

The lantern used the same fuel and wick arrangement as its sister the lamp. And like the chimney of the lamp, its glass globe demanded regular cleaning. A simple push upon the wire lever would raise it up to allow removal and a good cleaning by the same boy properly equipped with the ever-ready newspaper.

The lantern cast a pale glow, compared to the lamp. But it had a redeeming quality that lifted it beyond its sister, at least in my eyes. When I carried it to the stable, it cast me in a moving shadow well beyond my puny frame. With the aid of that simple lantern, I became a giant dancing across the snow, and only when the lantern and I entered the stable did the giant leave me. But he returned to dance with me on the way back to the house, to disappear again when I went inside. It was a magic lantern, to be sure.

One fine dark evening, a fancy sister joined the family lamp in the window. It had arrived all the way from Toronto, safely wrapped and boxed for the good people of Eaton's catalogue. Its name was Alladin, and it was the every essence of fine lighting. It boasted a chrome base that swept into a narrow stem, which blossomed out into a bowl to hold the oil. Over its wick was suspended a fine mesh mantle that when heated by the conic wick's flame, glowed white like a cosmic star. Truly, Alladin was a high-caste lamp, and the light of the mantle out-shone every other light in the house.

"We'll have to be careful with the Alladin lamp," warned Mother. "Mrs. Darling has one, and she says that the mantle is just like a white ash after the first time it's lit. She says one good shake, and it turns to dust. Remind me to order a spare one from Eaton's next week. Then we'll be ready, if somethin' happens." She ordered one the very next week. And although we were especially careful with Alladin, the mantle sometimes shattered into dust. But on such occasions we had a spare, ready and waiting. And if we didn't, then the good old table lamp came to our rescue.

Oh yes, Alladin had another feature that set her apart. Her tall, slender chimney was surrounded mid-way by a beautiful pink porcelain globe, held suspended by a brass wire frame. It cast a soft diffused light about the room, and when Mother was finally confronted by the electric light some years later, her first reaction was to regret the passing of her Alladin lamp.

All three of the lights in our family were dependent upon that magic oil that came from the ground. We bought coal oil by the gallon, and that can, although a simple container made from tin, was every bit as essential as the lamps it fed. Costing about twenty-five cents a gallon, coal oil could be purchased in the tiniest village, and a shopping trip was considered useless if the coal oil can was forgotten. That can and I had a love-hate relationship through the years. I was made to take a spoonful from it every spring, because of an odd adult belief that it was "good for what ails you," according to my Mother. And when we once rented a house on the outskirts of Huntsville, it was I who had to carry the can into the dreaded nest of the town mice to get it filled. The taunts of my electrically lit-up counterparts were brought on me by my telltale burden, which stuck like glue to my hand. Only when I arrived home safely did the coal oil can regain my respect. And in the quiet of the night, I blessed the can with its precious contents. I knew then that the only thing that stood between darkness and light for the Dennis family was not the lamps, or even the lantern. It was the oil that fuelled the flame. In time, our precious coal oil took on a new name. People called it kerosene. But that can in my treasure box still smells strongly of coal oil, and I'm not about to change its name.

The Exhibition

Almost three hundred years before I was born, Toronto's Exhibition grounds were already important. French fur traders had noticed that it was a gathering place for native people, so they built a fort there. They called it Fort Rouillé, which just happened to be the name of the Minister of Colonies in France. About sixty years later, when Toronto became the capital of Upper Canada, the grounds became part of the garrison fort to defend the newly born capital, which was known as York. Here it was that the Americans invaded in 1813. They burned the place down, and, as a final insult, they stole the mace, the traditional symbol of "people power," from its place in Upper Canada's government building. All seemed lost.

But not for long. In no time at all, Fort York was restored, and the land was at peace. York grew into the City of Toronto, itching to be the site of Canada's largest exhibition. It was a natural ambition, really. Agriculture was the main root of the country's economy, and fairs had already become a customary way of celebrating the bounty of the land. The first agricultural fairs moved about the province each year. But in 1879 it was decided that Toronto would be the annual site of the Agricultural Society's show. The City went full out to deserve the honour, and invited all and sundry to visit the "Toronto Exhibition." New buildings were erected on the very site that had earned its place in history more than a century earlier.

One building got special attention. It was the log home of a pioneer named Scadding, which was moved from its location by the Don River to a place of honour on the Exhibition grounds. It was still there when I visited the "Ex" as a boy. By then, of course, the fair had grown to earn the name "Canadian National Exhibition," and although it was not the only annual fair in the country, it was out to claim national fame and as far as I was concerned, that claim was entirely appropriate.

It was 1933, and I had never been to Toronto, or to any other place of importance—unless you were to consider Huntsville and Bracebridge important places. So when I heard my parents talking of the trip's possibility, I started a program of good behaviour. I knew about the Canadian National Exhibition, of course. Even a kid in Ullswater got to hear about such "national" extravaganzas. I never really expected to *go* to it, but it seemed that I was getting some unexpected help from my grandfather. James Dennis had gone to the United States after Grandma Dennis died, and apparently he did rather well there, while working for Dupont. Dad said that when Grandfather changed his money for Canadian dollars, he gained enough on the exchange to pay for a trip to Australia and New Zealand! He had now returned to Toronto, and had written to tell Dad that he would like to visit us.

"We could go down and get the old codger," said Dad, trying to sound reluctant. "If we did, we could pass by the Exhibition, and let the boys have a look around."

"And pigs can fly, too," answered Mother. "We're as poor as Job's turkey, and you talk of hitting out for Toronto! Still, I suppose if I took the money I've saved from selling baking to the tourists down at the lake ..." Then she thought of the possibility of having her father-in-law, probably rich enough to pay for his keep. "I guess we could make it, if you drive real slow," she said.

Now there were two things to look forward to: the Exhibition, and meeting grandfather Dennis. In 1930, Mother and Dad had gone to visit him in Flint, Michigan. They had taken Vernon with them, but I was left with the Darling family. I looked forward to the possibility of seeing him. Was he bigger than Dad, I wondered?

We left at about five o'clock one Saturday morning. Vernon and I fell asleep right away, and didn't wake up till dawn broke, just south of Orillia; and by that time we were so far from home that the countryside was foreign to us. The farms seemed larger than those at home, and many of them had windmills. Mailboxes dotted the roadside, and the constant traffic made the road seem crowded. Once we saw a sign saying "Clean Washrooms Ahead," and the number of billboards advertising accommodation for travellers grew so numerous that Vernon and I started to count them. "U-Cum Inn," "Nite Time Nook" and "Cozykabins" were among the many that we saw.

And poles! They lined both sides of the highway like soldiers joining us on our advance toward Toronto. And by the time we reached our goal, it seemed that we were surrounded by poles, wires and honking horns. And adding icing to the cake were the clanging streetcars with their humming rods of life reaching up to the cables overhead. For a ten-year-old confronting it for the first time, it was an awesome, almost frightening sight, and I began to doubt if I would have any astonishment left in me for the Exhibition.

But we weren't there yet. First, we had to go into the bowels of the city to get Granddad Dennis. Then I got another shock. In a house on River Street, he waited for us in the company of his ninety-year-old mother! This regal old matriarch had arrived from England by a separate set of circumstances, of which I knew nothing. It was enough for me to take it all in. First there was the long drive through the changing countryside, then more bustling traffic then I'd ever seen, now these aging relatives with their strange talk—and we were not even at the Exhibition yet! At least one question was answered. Granddad Dennis was taller than his son.

Then suddenly, there we were, in the midst of it, with its huge crowds, its massive, beautiful buildings, its aura of occasion. I wasn't worldly wise; but I knew one thing: I would never be the same again. It wasn't just one thing, either. It was the whole combination of sights and smells, of crowds of people all dressed in their Sunday best, the sounds of life inundating the atmosphere, all combining to sweep a country mouse right off his feet! And I was ever so glad when Mother sought out a grassy mound in full view of the lake, and sat us all down for our picnic lunch. Worthy soul that she was, she had come prepared, with chicken sandwiches, pickles, cookies and cold tea; and knowing that we were not up to sightseeing on an empty stomach, invited us to dig in.

Three things linger in my mind about that lunch so long ago. One was the sight of a small bi-plane flying lazily overhead, lingering as if to say, "Take a good look, Lloyd. I'm the first you've ever seen—but I won't be your last!" Another was the smell of cigar smoke, which drifted aimlessly past my nose from an old man passing by. And the third was the clacking sound of my grandfather's teeth as he ate his chicken sandwich. Of the myriad things that crowded in on my mind that day, a tiny plane, the smell of a cigar, and an old man's clacking teeth took first prize!

But my other senses would have their turn; and as we wound our way from one delight to another, we began to appreciate why the fair was so acclaimed. After all, the city fathers had been building the show for over fifty years, and now its grand buildings stretched along the shore of Lake Ontario in a splendid array of invitations to adventure.

Dad was more inclined toward the Manufacturers' Building, with its lavish displays of the modern industrial age. Mother was drawn to the Horticultural Building, with its abundance of flowers and plants. She promptly christened it the Flower Building. But she was most attracted to the Pure Food Building, which offered delights that even a master cook such as she could marvel at. As for Vernon and me, the Automotive Building was the winner. With its glistening displays of every automobile imaginable, new and old, it was hard to drag us away.

But we all fell in love with the Horse Palace and the Coliseum, with their endless variety of farm animals and produce. There, for the first time, we came face to face with the finest examples of life on the farm, from Percherons to pigs, from sheep to sheaves of grain. We even stood and stared at a life-sized cow, carved entirely from butter. "Sakes alive!" was all that Mother could manage.

The midway made my heart pound most of all. With its side shows of freaks and oddities, its games of chance and skill, and its pseudo-naughty magnetism, it was a "must" for all young folk. And when Mother took us for a ride on the large wooden whirling disc, I hung on for all my life, but was spun off anyway. I didn't know whether to laugh or cry.

We went into the Grandstand in the evening, as a final treat. "The Greatest Show on Earth" proved to be just that. A huge stage offered a melodrama complete with horsemen, musicians, chorus and tumbling stage props. And when the greatest—and only—shower of fireworks I had ever seen lit up the night, I was completely flabbergasted. The awful glory of it all lasted long after we gathered ourselves together and headed into the night—and home.

Huddled together with Grandfather Dennis and his travelling bag, we whispered together about the magic of it all. We were well beyond the city when we finally got around to wondering what our grandfather had brought us from his travels. We were both foolish enough to hope that our dream would come true. By some magic, he would announce that two bicycles were on their way, perhaps by train. But our hopes were dashed when, about an hour north of Toronto, he turned to us and said,

"Oh yes, boys, you must be wondering what souvenirs I have brought you from my travels. Well, I have them right here in my bag." And he reached into his luggage and, without ceremony, handed us each a jackknife. "Here you are," he said. "Be careful that you don't cut yourselves. They are quite sharp, you know."

They were quite sharp, in a manner of speaking; but they were not as sharp as that bicycle we had seen in Eaton's catalogue. But perhaps the catalogue didn't reach as far as New Zealand, so he wouldn't have seen it. Anyway, I was pleased with my knife, and fell asleep thinking about my adventures at the Exhibition, and the tales that I could tell the kids at school.

"They won't believe me when I tell them about a whole cow made of butter," I thought, and nodded off. And even I wouldn't have believed it if someone were to tell me that, within ten years, I would occupy a stall in that beautiful Horse Palace, along with thousands of other young fellows. By then, the Exhibition's buildings would have been directed to a far more sweeping and deadly purpose than entertaining a curious public, for they were converted to use by the Military. And half a century would go by before I would march proudly with my comrades of the First Canadian Parachute Battalion Association in the annual Warriors' Day Parade at the Canadian National Exhibition. I could still smell that cigar smoke and hear the clicking of Granddad's teeth, even over the glorious sound of the pipes and drums.

But those experiences had to take their turn. For the moment, I was deep in sleep; and Mother had a hard job waking me when we reached home in the wee hours of the morning.

Here Today—Gone Tomorrow

This tale had begun with a handshake. Bert Simms offered Dad a job at his budding business operation on Skeleton Lake. It included a small lumber mill and a tourist complex called Simolean Beach, which was a courageous attempt to attract city folk in the face of the coming depression of the thirties. Several summer residents had already established themselves in cottages on the rim of the bay, and Simms saw his enterprise as a logical extension of the net to capture tourists.

"You could scale lumber for me, Alf," explained Simms. "And you could be my bookkeeper over at the lodge. I'm a little short of cash, but I'll tell you what I'll do. I'll give you a couple of acres up the road from the lake, and enough lumber to build yourself a house. I think that it's a good deal. You get a place for your family to call 'home,' and I get your brains to keep my numbers straight. What do you say? Can we shake on it?"

Dad shook Simms' hand. The deal was sealed.

We were living in a tiny rented house at Martin's Siding, about twenty miles away. My brother and I, our dog Jumbo and even our horse Jessie were quite contented with our lot, and as far as we were concerned, life was just one adventure after another. But for Mother, it was different. Caught on the merry-go-round of Dad's search for work, she was constantly on the move. She called herself a "homebody"; yet yearned to have a place of her very own. But hard times were upon us, and the possibility of a Dennis house seemed remote indeed. Thus it was that when Dad came home and broke the news, she literally picked him up and kissed him.

"Just think of it!" she exclaimed, "Our own house! Our very own house! At Skeleton Lake, you say? Why, I can sell my Parker House rolls to the tourists, and we can have a garden, and you, Lloyd, you can sell flowers to 'em! Alf, you get goin' on that house, and we'll start packin'. Boys you get off down to Carl Brown's store and ask him to save any boxes that come his way. We'll be needin' them."

A new world awaited us at Skeleton Lake. Located less than a mile from the shore, the house stood near the road, and soon grew to include a stable for Jessie, and a root-house for vegetables. Our "family" grew too. A cow named Beauty was joined by two piglets called Jimmy and Jamie. A flock of hens moved into the hen house, while an equal number of turkeys roamed the small clearing. And giving life to it all was our mother, who brought such a spirit to the place that it took on a life of its own. Indeed, before long, she had reached out to claim new friends and neighbours, just as she had at Aspdin and Martin's Siding.

But there were two sides to our world. One offered the rural families of Ullswater, where names like Bunn, Creasor, Beathune, Olsen, Lee and Tibble dotted the landscape. They were the steadfast roots upon whom Mother thrived throughout the year. But the summer side of her world offered a different face. Here she made friends with cottage folk with names like Catlin, Philkin and Switzer. They sprang up like summer flowers each year, and were swept up by the magic of Mother's Parker House rolls, muffins, pies and other culinary delights that emerged from her modest kitchen. In no time at all, she and Dad were regular players at the Catlin card table, while Vernon and I ogled their visiting granddaughters. And we were happy to sell flowers from our garden to these city folk—as long as at least a part of the proceeds could lead to an ice cream cone or a candy bar found among the treasures at the local lodge.

Vegetables from the Dennis garden also found their way to the cottage tables, until it seemed that Mother was bringing more money to the table than Dad. Then, when she began to take in laundry, she was the clear breadwinner. But Dad offered no complaint. After all, he had already contributed a large share to our fortune with the shake of the hand! Even Jessie was part of the action. When summer came, she was rented to the lodge to join the horses at the riding stable; and many a southerner enjoyed the thrill of a ride on her sleek back, adorned as it was with a western saddle.

Of course, being children of the "help," we weren't allowed to play on the beach with tourist children. But we didn't mind. We preferred the mill pond, where we could swim naked with our own kind. I must confess that on several occasions I stole away to play with Georgina Switzer, and even provided my own doll—which I still have, by the way. But this friendship was a secret which I kept from my friends at the mill pond.

With the fading of summer, the tourists disappeared like falling leaves, and we would turn to our real world in Ullswater, which had little to offer, either in excitement or money. But it offered a wealth of adventure in other ways. With the tourists gone, Jessie returned to our stable, and our vegetables moved into the root house for the coming winter. Wood was cut, feed stored, and Vernon and I made ready for school, equipment for which included pencil box, writing tools and a new scribbler. Greater priority was given to the hoop and stick which would provide our means of transportation. Then, armed with the sling-shot that every country boy considered essential, we were on our way. (In Muskoka, we called it a catapult, or "caddy.")

With the arrival of winter, our hoops surrendered to our skis, which were joined by long underwear, mitts and high rubbers. We were then ready for whatever winter had to offer.

So was Mother. She was as adept with the needle as she was with the stove; and she could hook rugs, knit socks or stitch a quilt with the best of them. I never knew my mother to read a book (other than Eaton's catalogue), but I never saw her hands idle. She was cooking, preserving, knitting or sewing all the time. And when winter came, we were glad of it. Everything, from berries to rhubarb to catfish and beef found its way into jars in the root house; and on many a bleak winter night in the midst of a country of growing poverty, the Dennis family ate like royalty.

Our dog Jumbo worked, too. Mr. Olsen, the blacksmith, made a fine set of miniature logging sleighs for us, and we would hitch up our dog and draw wood for the coming spring. While Dad whittled spiles from pieces of cedar, we piled the wood in a convenient place in the bush, and waited for the season of sap. And when it came, the whole family moved industriously into the making of maple syrup. One more delight was added to the Dennis larder.

The school was small by today's standards with only about sixteen pupils. Still, it offered up some good friends who are treasured to this day. Situated about a mile from home, it was the centre of interest for the community, and was certainly a major force in our young lives, which seemed locked forever in a part of the world that was both rich and poor. But as the clouds of the Great Depression spread across the sky, they even dimmed the bright days of Ullswater and Skeleton Lake. Bert Simms was one of the first to feel its effect. As business faltered in the cities to the south, fewer cars found their way to the magic of Muskoka, and for the first time, the lodge at Simolean Beach had rooms to spare. Cottagers kept coming, but their visits were fewer, and farther apart. The mill fell idle, its bright new lumber bereft of buyers. Dad fell idle too, with no lumber to scale and few numbers to keep in the lodge's books. He sought local work, and even found some on a nearby road project. But when that, too, came to an end, the Dennis family, poor but proud, found itself resorting to the dreaded voucher that was a weekly pittance paid to people on relief.

"Never mind," said Mother, with her usual stoicism. "We may be down, but we're not out."

Poor woman. She didn't know how wrong she was. When I stopped at the Bunn farm to pick up the mail one day, I was handed a letter. Long and business-like, it was addressed to "Mr. Alfred Dennis, Esquire," and came from the Ginsberg brothers in Huntsville, who held the mortgage on Simms' property. It carried a fateful message.

The mortgage on the Simms' property had been foreclosed, and the Dennis family had thirty days to "vacate the premises." The added order that we could "take nothing nailed down" only added salt to the wound. With her world suddenly collapsing around her, Mother put her hands to her face and cried.

"Whatever will we do, AIf?" she sobbed.

There was little to do. A plea fell on deaf ears. "You had a handshake, but you have no deed," was the reply from the mortgagee. "You have thirty days to move."

And so the Dennis family was scattered like dust in the wind. With our few belongings on a borrowed truck, we were a mile up the road before I missed my dog. "Where's Jumbo?" I asked plaintively.

"I'm sorry, son," answered Dad. "We have no house to go to, so I asked Mr. Beathune to shoot him."

I was too overcome to notice that Mother too, had to part with a beloved possession. There was no room on the truck for her box stove, so it was abandoned with other refuse behind the house.

Today, a youth camp sits on the shore of the lake. It turned out that neither our house nor the land on which it stood was needed. Our land still stands empty by the side of the road. But our house is long gone. Soon after we left, some enterprising body moved it two miles down the road, where it finally burned to the ground. Perhaps it is just as well, I am sure that it was haunted by my mother's broken heart.

Jessie's Tale

I was born on the farm of Louis Grimes, in Allensville. I don't remember much about it, but I heard my masters say that it was a cold April night in 1924. They also said that I was a pretty little bay colt, and that I should grow up to be a great driver.

Now, for people who know little about horses, let me explain that a driver is not a person who drives the buggy, but the horse that pulls it. And that's just what I grew up to be, a good driver. It was my profession, you might say; and be it buggy, democrat or cutter, I pulled with the best of them. Once I was broken in, I never looked back.

In 1929, Louis Grimes died, and I found a new life. His wife Rebecca (better known as "Granny" because she had so many grandchildren) went to live in Martin's Siding with her daughter Bessie. Naturally, I went with her, complete with my harness, my blanket and my buggy. They said that we'd come back for the cutter in the winter. So I said good-bye to my friends in Allensville, and off I went to my new home.

Martin's Siding was only about three miles away, but to me it felt as though I had moved to another world. There was no barn, no other animals, not even a proper stable; and I had every reason to hang my head as Alf Dennis led me into a little shed and tied me up in a makeshift stall. As he took off my harness and bridle I could have cried. And when he patted my head, I looked into his eyes and tried to show him how forlorn I felt. He must have known, for he gave me another pat and said, "There, there, Jess. We'll take good care of you—and just think! You're the only girl in the family!"

Things got better. I could graze freely on the small field nearby, and sometimes they would hitch me up to the buggy and off we'd go to visit friends in Aspdin, where I heard that Lloyd was born just a year before me. We'd clatter along the gravel road, and always remember to turn into the creek where I could get a drink. Then across the creek and back to the road I'd go with the Dennis family hanging on behind.

When winter came, they took me down to get the cutter. And I'll tell you, those trips to Aspdin were fun for all of us. We'd swish along through the darkness, with the bells on my shafts ringing merrily, my passengers bundled up in the buffalo robe and warmed blocks of wood wrapped in blankets at their feet. Clods of snow would fly from my feet and smack against the cutter's dashboard; and sometimes I'd even break wind, much to the boys' delight.

When we reached our destination, I would be covered with a blanket and wait patiently while the family played cards or danced in the community hall. Sometimes I would doze a bit; but when Alf said "Giddap, Jesse!" I was off and running. It always seemed easier going home.

I don't know what happened, but about a year later they drove me to my new home in Ullswater, a house near Skeleton Lake. It stood on the edge of the bush about half a mile from the beach, and had a small stable, big enough for me and a couple of cows. We all settled in to my new surroundings, and over the next year I was joined by a cow, two pigs, and about twenty hens. Even though they couldn't speak my language, they gave a great lift to my spirits. On many a night we would chat away just as if we knew what everyone was talking about.

Then my buggy went missing, and an old car appeared in the yard. I put two and two together. The buggy was no longer needed, which meant that I would have the summers off. I relished the thought of long lazy summer days grazing to my heart's content in the verdant fields nearby. What a life!

But it wasn't quite like that. Young Lloyd had learned to ride me bareback, and all too often he would fasten my bridle, and off we'd go to get the mail, visit Clyde, or go down to the forbidden territory called the "Beach." Simolean Beach Resort was there. Since Alf Dennis worked there, Lloyd was a child of the help, and not welcome.

But I was. As it turned out, I ended up being rented to the Resort each summer as a saddle horse. Poor Lloyd! Bereft of his horse during summer, he could only look longingly as I was ridden grandly up the road past his house!

In the winter, I was back to work with the cutter. On many a stormy night I would be off to the village store at Raymond, taking the family to buy supplies. Often the drifts were deep enough to make me struggle, but we always made it through. I was always rather proud of that.

Then something happened. Suddenly, the Dennis family had to

leave their house. Jumbo the dog was shot, and I was sold to Mr. Hammell, over on Three Mile Lake. There I blended in with other horses on the Hammell farm and slowly aged away. I died in 1940, still fondly remembering my glory days with the Dennis family.

From Horses' Heaven, my spirit looks down upon the place I used to call home, and note that the Hammells I knew are gone, and only Lloyd remains of the Dennis family. I wonder if he remembers the time he rode me between the fence and the telephone pole—and got swept from my back! And I see that there's a golf course near the farm where I spent my last days. They call it "Diamond in the Ruff." I think that's what I was, too.

Help!

The thousands of people who annually arrived on Muskoka's summer doorstep during the heyday of hotels made for good business. Many of them were wealthy and accustomed to the "finer things of life"; and they certainly expected that their holiday experience would offer nothing less. The proprietors knew this of course, and went out of their way to anticipate every need or whim that their guests presented.

Owners who also served as operators of their establishments were most tuned to meet such requirements. They lived on the premises, and were familiar with the availability of local human resources that they could call upon for summer employment. They also knew "by the grapevine" where they could search beyond the area for the most suitable help, which was often the city of Toronto. Many a maid sought work in "holiday heaven" during the summer months, and only returned when the guests departed—often on the same boat!

The "help," as these workers were called, came in great variety of expertise, from bellhops to chamber maids, baggage handlers, boatmen, handymen, carpenters and cleaners. High on the hierarchy were the cooks, of course; and many hotels were known for their culinary prowess—or the lack of it. It was a wise proprietor who put "Chef" on the top of his list when searching for staff.

It was customary to maintain a proper distance between guests and staff. After all, these people paid to come, and deserved a certain degree of royal treatment. And that demanded that people "below the salt" be recognized for what they were. They were servants, members of the help; and good ones knew their place. It became the custom to recognize this condition as a new social order that came with the resort business in Muskoka; and as the custom grew, natives and visitors came to know their place. In many establishments, rules and regulations governing behaviour of the help were firmly established, lest there be an offensive breach. Modes of dress and decorum were established, and woe to those who failed to heed.

With the advent of the automobile, guests began to arrive in fine cars driven by chauffeurs, some of whom where black. They were not even allowed at Bigwin Inn, and had to be quartered in cabins provided at a lesser hotel elsewhere. Of course, they were not allowed near the beach!

But not all hotels were so severe in drawing lines between the helper and the helped. Some establishments, like WaWa, across the bay from Bigwin Inn, and Wigwassan Lodge on Lake Rosseau, were examples of a more relaxed atmosphere between guests and staff. Such owners were convinced that a degree of familiarity didn't necessarily breed contempt. Indeed, it could provide a bond that was mutually beneficial. And today's recollections from both sides seem to prove them right.

My experiences in this episode of Muskoka history were vicarious, and came late in the day. My parents always spoke warmly of their brief but poignant service at Beaumaris, where they met and married. But to me it was ancient history, before the Great War, for Heaven's sake! At the time of their telling, it was in the thirties, and we were far removed from a romance that bloomed in some old hotel. Why, even I knew that the summer parades to the grand hotels was down to its last wobbly walk-ins. Oh, there were still some around; but the advent of the automobile and the aircraft had forever changed the habit of the tourist, and even homey hotels like Deerhurst had fallen on hard times. The Depression didn't help matters, and even the cottage crowd grew thinner as the hard times of the thirties took their toll.

By that time the Dennis family was clearly labeled "help" in the tourist industry. I went with Mother when she became cook at Burnbrae Lodge, right across from Deerhurst on Peninsula Lake; and while Dad fixed docks for cottage owners, I found out first-hand what it was like being on the "other end of the stick" in the tourist business. Mother worked for the Wares, who were the owner-proprietors of the lodge. They were good people, and Mother enjoyed working for them. But, looking at lodges through the back door certainly gave a different perspective about being on the "help" end of things; and I, for one, learned a new meaning for the word. It seems to have been derived from the American use of the term "help," which means "a farm labourer or domestic servant." It had nothing to do with being a "good Samaritan," and I had to behave as if I understood that.

Of course, this was not the first time I had been on the side of "the help" in the tourist trade. At Simolean Beach I learned which side of my bread was buttered, and as children of the help, we stayed within our bounds. But now I was going on thirteen, and was more acutely aware of the impact of social restriction. Though those croquet balls just cried to be hit with the waiting mallet, I was forced to ignore their call, even when the guests had long since lost interest. I could help to tighten the badminton net, but it was "hands off" that racket! And those horseshoes! The closest I ever got to them was to rake the mounds around the stake—after the guests had left for the day.

But one day I was offered an experience that was so burned into my mind that I still recall it in detail. A group of "the anointed" were about to take a ride in the Burnbrae launch, and they spied me looking wistfully at them from behind a tree on the bank. One generous soul called out.

"Aren't you the cook's son? Would you like to go for a boat ride with us?"

I was down to the dock and into the boat in seconds. And for the next hour I had the most luxurious ride of my life. When the lady in charge invited me to enjoy a slice of watermelon, I really felt as though I'd crossed the Great Divide. Having never eaten watermelon before, I thought that it tasted a little strange; but if this was the price one paid for being a tourist it was well worth it. When I came back to earth, Mother asked me where I'd been.

"I've been boating with the tourists," I said loftily. "And I even ate a slice of watermelon." "Well you're back on the side of the help again," she reminded me. "We're not here to ride around in boats, you know. Go bring in some wood."

Which is exactly what I did.

We Have a New Boy at School Today

It's not easy planting new roots. The soil has to adjust to this intruder and move over to make room for it. And the root, which never asked to be planted in this unknown soil in the first place, is certain to feel a bit apprehensive. Of course, had it sprouted there from seed, it would feel quite at home; but to be stuck in the dirt like a stick—well, it's a traumatic experience, to say the least.

I felt that trauma nine times when I was a schoolboy; and although the horror of those experiences was sharpened by my sensitivity and imagination, they were nonetheless real to me. Even today as I look back upon them, they need little fanning to bring them to a glow.

Take that first day at Ullswater, for instance. I started out with fear and trepidation, and I didn't have long to wait. Clyde, on ascertaining that my middle name was Arthur, took great delight in repeatedly calling me "Art the Fart" on the way to school. And just as I felt whittled down to nothing, there she was at the door. She may not have been unduly large by adult standards; but to me, she appeared to be about as large as a human being could get. She wore a purple suit, which didn't help matters, somehow.

It got worse. Suddenly, shortly after opening exercise she said, "Stand up, Lloyd." I stood—and all eyes turned on me. I can still see them, with a half a yard of finger up their noses, waiting with bated breath for the lion to pounce upon its victim. And when she said, "Read!" you could almost feel the delighted anticipation of the crowd. I stood there, pleading wordlessly for God to strike me dead as I looked at the designated page in Second Book. It was page 26 and was entitled "Lucy of the Lighthouse." As if to further my fears, it showed a young girl on the shore of the ocean before a lighthouse on the craggy shore.

I looked at Lucy, at the purple suit, and then at the class of picking noses. It was too much. I just let go. Through an inch of long underwear, two inches of breeks and all the way down my leg, the water went to form a puddle on the floor—right under the eyes of my nemesis.

"Lloyd! Look at what you've done! Naughty boy! You stay in at recess and clean that up with salt and water!"

I didn't realize until sometime later what a redundant order that was. I had already provided the salt! All that I needed was the water and soap. But I did what I was told, all the while praying for God to strike me dead.

Moving to Utterson put me in double jeopardy. Not only was I entering a virtual city, with four stores, ice cream parlour, blacksmith shop, garage, post office and community hall, among other urban niceties, it was also the home of my cousin Sethie. His father owned the garage, and Sethie owned a bicycle. And lest one assume that this would ease my entry into this new world, let me hasten to say that a joyful greeting was not forthcoming.

The fact that the school had two rooms, indoor plumbing and electric lights was overwhelming enough; but to see Sethie with his bicycle practically ignoring his newly arrived cousin was a blow that I didn't need. And when someone egged Dalton on to pick a fight with me, I was in a desperate state. They stood in a circle on "main street," with Dalton and me in the middle. And like Roman spectators in the ancient Coliseum, they called for blood.

Dalton and I took the stance of pugilists, each hoping that the other would run home. We pranced and lunged ferociously, being careful not to land the first blow, until finally some adult came down the street and closed the Coliseum down. The crowd dispersed, and the two champions were led away by their separate supporters.

Leaving for lunch one day I saw Sethie's bicycle by the fence, and rode home proudly. Upon my return, Sethie was waiting for me. With a few choice words of abuse, he slapped my face for my thievery. Then, as if nothing had happened, he asked if I would like to go to his house after school. Four o'clock saw two young fellows on one bicycle, speeding down the hill on their way to Sethie's house. They played checkers till five o'clock, and Lloyd vowed that he would never take Sethie's bike again.

Ever so gradually, I began to feel comfortable in this new ground; and when we put on the Christmas concert in the Community Hall, I recited Lochinvar with all the bravado of the original hero. When Dalton and Sethie allowed that I had done a good job, I was quite content to stay in Utterson forever.

It was not to be. The following May I was suddenly uprooted and glumly faced the prospect of being "new boy" once again.

The Canal School was great. Situated on the canal between Fairy and Peninsula lakes, it was an attractive one-room affair with a young male teacher and about twenty pupils. Mr. Laycock greeted me warmly, and it made my day. Within a week, I was accepted as a friend by just about everyone in the class; and when school closed in

June, I went home almost reluctantly. I knew that I would not be coming back.

The Fall of 1936 found me boarding with the Earl family, in Aspdin, the village of my birth. This presented me with another case of double jeopardy—homesickness and sleeping with Bill and Sid!

Dame fortune smiled upon me at the Aspdin school. The Earl's were loving hosts, and many of the children were known to me from earlier days. Mr. Hammell was an engaging teacher who took note of my rather itinerant history and made suitable allowances. And to top it off, Bill Earl let me join him in driving a calf about four miles to the Stisted Fall Fair. I think it was during that meandering trip that I determined never to become a farmer.

It was Falkenburg's turn in October when Mother took me with her to the Moores', where she was to cook for them at the mill. On my first walk to school up the old Muskoka Road I met the teacher, Helvi Macki, and by the time we arrived, I was in love with her. The rest was easy. The Forth boys became fellow hunters as we sought out partridges with our catapults and, led by Miss Macki, explored unknown regions in the Ontario Public School Geography.

The Falkenburg adventure was over by Christmas. My parents and brother headed for wilderness country, to a logging camp in Ravensworth, a tiny settlement just west of Algonquin Park. Mother would cook, Dad would be the scaler and timekeeper, and Vernon would cut logs with the other men. I was assigned to a more difficult task. "You will board with Hazel and Pat, and go to the town school in Huntsville," she ordered. "And don't put on that long face. It won't help you none. And mind! I want you to be a good boy, and do what Hazel says. We'll be out in the Spring. Then we'll all be together again."

One can only imagine that first walk to school, on sidewalks in rubbers and breeks, for Pete's sake! When I got to the school, it was so big I was almost afraid to go in; and when I did, I headed straight for the toilets. There, to my amazement was a row of what looked like little bathtubs, standing on their ends. The odd one was occupied, so

I stood in one too. But I was too nervous to use the facility. As I stood there trying to look nonchalant, a boy named Louis occupied the one on my right. After a few cutting remarks, he slapped my face! It was some time before we became friends, and it took even longer for me to appreciate that the greeting was a ritual that most country mice experienced when they entered town mouse territory. But the worst was yet to come.

"Stand up, Lloyd!" The teacher seemed eighteen feet tall. He wore thinly framed glasses and a look of all-knowing severity. I stood up in my breeks and rubbers midst a sea of long pants and skirts, waiting for the blow to come.

"Where were you in History in the last school which you attended?"

Where was I in History? Why, I could hardly remember the name of the last school. I had been in about five schools in the past year. But I knew that he needed an answer, so I blurted out, "Page 16!"

"Page 16?" he repeated contemptuously. "Why, you'll never catch up to this class with roller skates on!" The whole class laughed, while I sat down in humiliation. With that one remark, the teacher had seared my soul, and left a mark that is there to this day.

Three days later I went to the good and kindly Hazel, and mustering all my courage, said "I'd like to run away."

"I know," said Hazel. "And I know who you want to run to. Your mother. Why, you can't fool me, Lloyd. I've heard you up there cryin' in your bed! Well, you picked the right day to run. The Northland comes through tonight. You catch her, and get off at Scotia Junction, transfer to the log train when it comes through on its way to Algonquin Park, and get off at Ravensworth. You'll be with your mother by one in the morning. Now pack your bag and get ready. Pat will walk you to the train."

Which is what I did. And although I didn't expect to find a school back there in the wilderness, my surprised mother had me off and running to it the very next morning.

The camp broke up in May; but that's another story.

Shangri-La In the Bush

One would think that, compared with Huntsville, Ravensworth had very little to offer a young boy in the winter of 1937. It was a mere speck of humanity on the edge of the wilderness, where its tiny school, railway station and one old house were the sole signs of habitation, along with the recently opened Muskoka Wood logging camp. It boasted no stores, electric lights, indoor toilets or running water. There was no need for streets, for there was no traffic. No sidewalks invited folks to gather and gossip, and no policeman enforced the law. It was, indeed, a lonely place by ordinary standards; and when the lamps were blown out at night, there was little sign of life, save for the wisps of smoke rising from the bunkhouse and the cookhouse.

I had already tasted the "delights" of town life and found it wanting. No amount of sophisticated urbanity, even that offered by the beautiful town of Huntsville, could warm my soul after my searing experience on that first day of school. Now I was about to test the only other alternative open to me: that silent cluster of dark buildings that lay beside the tracks where I got off the train.

Certainly, the abode that greeted me after the walk up from the station was not imposing. Mother and Dad shared a bunk at the back of the cookhouse, complete with a straw tick that served as a mattress. Rough shelves on the wall and one chair were the only other furnishings in their bedroom. The rest of the space in the building was taken up by the more important furniture for which it was intended. Long tables and benches reached to the business end of Mother's work area, which held a huge stove, woodbox and sink. Sturdy clusters of shelves and bins were stocked with provisions, and the whole place was lit by the lamps I knew so well from other days. As I crawled up into that top bunk above my parents, the straw tick rustled as if to welcome me home. I had been scolded for running away, to be sure. But that was behind me, and soon I was asleep.

I woke up in the Land of Logs. Logging camps in Muskoka had been around much longer than I had. In fact, they had been in this region of Canada almost from the beginning of its recorded history. A century before I arrived upon the scene, the production of lumber from the area had sown the seeds of industry and settlement, and the town of Huntsville was one of many that had sprung from the products of the surrounding forests. To many, they were known as "lumbering" towns; and the move into the camps was an annual ritual for many workers. I was a "product" of one of these earlier camps, and although circumstances had moved me around like a whirling dervish since then, I was well steeped in the language and the ethics of the bush. So the world in which I found myself that morning was more in keeping with my experience than the world from which I had escaped. The straw tick was strange; but it had a welcome feel, and I was content.

I didn't know it then, of course, but the adventurous era of the camps was nearing its end. The forests of this new land had given up most of their treasure by the 1930s, and the lumbering business was slowly giving way to the tourist trade. The Booth Railway, which had dropped me off in Ravensworth, was itself on dying wheels. Built against tremendous odds by the enterprising John Booth in the late 1800s, it had run from Parry Sound to Ottawa, and although it had carried a variety of goods over the years, its chief reason for existence was the movement of timber, in one form or another. The line was sold to the Grand Trunk in 1904, and by the time I was born in 1923, it was owned by the Canadian National Railways. But when a trestle collapsed in Algonquin Park, it was never repaired. The once famous line was past its glory, and when it assisted me in my escape in 1937, it was nearing its end as a means of timber transportation. Thank goodness it was still alive when I needed it!

The beauty of Ravensworth—or the lack of it—depended upon your point of view. If you were one of the few Finnish-Canadian settlers whose farms were scattered among the surrounding hills, you found it a remote but satisfying reminder of the old country. If you were a member of the French-Canadian family living up by the trestle on the railway track, you thanked God for the farmers whose few children at least provided a need for a school. If you happened to be a worker in the camp, you were likely to see Ravensworth as a frigid hole in the bush full of the endless slog of work fit only for horses, punctuated regularly by hearty meals and draughty bunks of straw. Except for the cook, there wasn't a woman for miles. And when that cook began to look attractive, you knew that the end was near!

If you were the cook, you had a different view of Ravensworth entirely. You rose daily in the middle of the night to set the bread and rolls. Then you napped till just before dawn, when you got up to set out the lunches, and cook breakfast for about forty starving men. These were no ordinary breakfasts, either. They included meat and potatoes, corn syrup and even pies, which had to be baked each day. The men drank their tea from granite mugs and ate from plates made from the same material. Except for the clatter of these dishes, silence reigned, for custom decreed that breakfast provided no time for idle talk. Next came cleanup time, and time to get ready for the feast at the closing of the day, which often surpassed in quantity most Canadian suppers. When the last of the men had left the table, you began all over again. And, as if the day had not already been long enough, there were often night crews appearing at the stroke of midnight, attacking the table as if they had not eaten for days!

On top of all this, there were your husband's needs, for he, too, depended upon you, not only for food but for laundry and advice, as well. And lord save us! That's your son coming up from the train! As if you didn't already have enough to do!

If you were the teacher, you often thought of those days when Ravensworth boasted a mill and had earned the status of a village. But now it was in its dying days, and you were thankful to have the nine children that were left. You welcomed them each day, though you knew full well that Parcelia and Arni were now in the Entrance Class, and would leave in June. You were pleased, therefore, when young Lloyd came knocking. He made one more, if only until Spring, when the camp broke up. Mrs. Dennis was a great cook, and good company. How nice it was to join her on an evening for a mug of tea and a chat. You would miss her when she left for home.

And if you were Tom Malloy, you were that delightful Irish-Canadian who served as flunkey for the cook, all-round handyman, chore-boy, and the man who met the train. You always met the train for the camp's mail, any provisions that it might disgorge—and for a jug of wine for your private consumption. That wine was your weakness. But beyond that you were a great, good, gentle man who warmed the soul of the dreary workers around you. You saw Ravensworth as your theatre of the moment; but when you took Lloyd off the train that cold night in January and ushered him into the presence of his mother, neither of you knew that the two of you would form a curious bond of brotherhood that the boy would remember throughout his days. For he was hungry for companionship and good advice, and you had plenty of both to offer him.

Listen to those horses, stomping and snorting in the stable! Some saw them as the treasure of the camp, for without them and their sturdy strength, the operation would not exist. A fine mixture of Clydesdales, Percherons and Belgians they were, each fed and coddled by their teamsters who, through everlasting care, earned with their horses the respect of the camp. It was the teamsters who were the last to seek the comfort of the bunkhouse at the end of the day, and the first to rise and tend their charges before breakfast in the morning. My brother Vernon was an assistant teamster, and I was proud of him for that. He and his senior teamsters never thought much about Ravensworth, for they were too busy looking after their horses to give the environment much attention.

And Dad? I doubt if he saw Ravensworth beyond a place that provided a living for his family. He still suffered from the loss of his home in Ullswater; but at Ravensworth he had regained a bit of self-respect, serving as the camp's bookkeeper and manager of the "van." This was a tiny store, which was sparsely stocked with goods intended to meet the immediate needs of the men. Socks, shirts, mitts, tobacco and liniment were popular items in the store. But his chief tasks were to keep track of the men's time upon which their wages were based, to record the shipment of logs, and to make certain that the provisions of the camp were properly supplied. Mother made sure that he was not negligent in that regard.

As for me, Ravensworth was a veritable Shangri-La. Already safe in the bosom of my family, the rest was a piece of cake, as they say. I met the teacher at the school's door and she never did ask me where I was in History. She dismissed my left-handedness with a nod of the head and hardly noticed my poor writing skills.

"There are five Finnish-Canadian children here, and four French-Canadians. I'm Irish myself, and Lord knows what you are. But come on in, we're like a little League of Nations, aren't we?"

I fell in love with her right off the bat; and before the end of the day I had embraced them all as my new friends. The bond grew by leaps and bounds as I was woven with care into this bracing new environment. Sometimes in the evening, the teacher would share a precious moment over a mug of tea with Mother, and often Tom would join them, regaling them with his homespun wit. Dressed in overalls, grey shirt, complete with grimy red tie, suit-coat and fedora, his regalia stood out in this harsh environment. But for as long as I knew him, I never saw him dressed otherwise. It was the uniform of the moment for this odd and lovely man. I think that my mother and the teacher thought that he dressed up for them!

So the days were spent by the men in the bush, where they were already working at the break of day. They cut the logs and horses pulled them to the skidways, where they were loaded onto sleighs. These were pulled along the draw-roads to the waiting railway cars. Here, other skills were applied to load the logs and make them ready for their last ride.

Meanwhile, I was attacking the mysteries of senior fourth with my comrades, Parcelia and Arni. On Saturday I would help with the chores, which mainly consisted of getting water from the well and stocking the wood-box of the cookhouse. It was during these times that I gathered endless bits of wisdom and humour from my dear friend Tom.

My new friends scoffed at my "store-bought" skis, which I had brought with me. They were a far cry from the home-made beauties with which Arni and the others were equipped. But in no time at all, one of their fathers presented me with a real pair of Finnish-style skis, complete with rawhide harness! There I was, still a "new boy," and already I was one of them!

More was to follow. It was their custom to have a sauna, or steam bath, every Saturday night, and I was invited regularly to ski out to one of their homes and partake of this invigorating ritual. It was the real thing, too, complete with water thrown on hot rocks, the testing of one's will to sit on the top-most bench, and the thrashing of one's body with birch switches. Then it was out to roll naked in the snow before being served with coffee and cookies. Skiing home with one of the younger workers of the camp, I looked up at the shifting glory of the northern lights, heard the howling of the wolves in the bush, and felt fulfilled.

As the days grew longer, I knew that the end was near. Already able to say a few things in French and Finnish, thanks to my new friends, I felt as one with them. All the rigours of the difficult struggle experienced by the adults in the camp were washed away in my personal flirtation with carefree life. For me, Ravensworth was all that a boy could ask for. And I had my new skis, the pride of my life. I willed the snow to stay.

Finally the dark day came. I stood on the platform of the station and waited with my mother for the train. My brother would drive a team out, so he came to see us off. So did Parcelia and her sister Lucille—and naturally, Tom Malloy was there too. I never saw him again. As if prepared to meet my Maker, I was all dressed up, not at all in keeping with my life at my Shangri-La. But mother thought it more fitting, somehow. After all we were heading back to Huntsville!

Sadly, the cost of my blissful period of joy in the bush became known when mother received her pay for her winter's work. Her employer had deducted thirty dollars to cover the cost of my board. I wish that I had eaten more!

The Blue Parcel

As I marched forward to do battle with the 1937 Entrance Examinations, those formidable bastions that had to be conquered before entering high school, I already felt defeated. I had been in four schools that year, and was about to enter my fifth. This new teacher would have to be a dauntless leader if she were to ensure my survival, let alone my victory.

Edith Goodwin was indeed dauntless. From the moment I met her, in her grey skirt and pink blouse, I knew that I was in the hands of an expert.

"My, you have been around, haven't you Lloyd? Well, never mind. We'll get right to it, and by the time those old exams show up, we'll be more than ready."

In those days, the Examinations were written by children from town and surrounding country schools. Town students, reflecting the inequality of the day, could by-pass the ordeal, on the recommendation of their school. Rural children had to write, regardless of their ability. But the medals awarded by local notables were a sufficient enticement to attract even those who were not obligated to write, and each year a number of Huntsville's best were there, seeking the ultimate battle trophy.

The struggle came at the end of June, and was actually a three-day conflict. I approached the field cautiously, lest a sudden movement would jar my brains and spill their contents on the road. I walked in a daze, half in the reality of education, and half in a fantasy of war, which I so often created in times of difficulty. Then I was there, in the sterile classroom, seated silently with the others.

Bang! We were over the top at nine o'clock, and into the first bloody skirmish, which happened to be a number of seasoned questions from the Arithmetic division.

"A man bought a house for $6,000.00. His yearly taxes are at the rate of 30 mills on the dollar on an assessment of $4,000.00. Insurance costs for the year are $18.00 and the yearly repairs cost $102.00. What must be the monthly rental of the house, in order that the owner may receive an annual return of 8 per cent on his investment of $6,000.00 after paying all expenses?"

Miss Goodwin had reviewed methods of killing such questions just last week. Bang! Dead! It was worth fourteen points. On to the next.

Thus the battle raged for three days. Arithmetic, Composition, Geography, Grammar, History, Literature, Reading, Spelling and Writing. Hour after hour they presented themselves. And the scratching of pens was the only noise of conflict. On occasion there would be the scrape of a foot, or a sigh from the mortally wounded; other than that, and the periodic clearing of Mr. Calderwood's throat, there was quiet. Then suddenly, the startling call of "Time!" would end the struggle, often with the warriors still engaged. We would drag ourselves home exhausted, to lick our wounds and prepare for the next attack.

Finally the war was over. The long meandering struggle that had taken me through nine schools on my way to the Entrance Examinations had come to an end. Whether it had ended in disaster or success would not be known until the judges examined our battle records, and announced the names of the victors and the fallen. We would have to wait.

Miss Goodwin knew how troops should retire from battle. Rest and recreation was the order of the day. Without waiting for the outcome to be announced, she went the second mile. She loaded us all into her brother's panel truck, and off we went to Callender to see the famous Quints.

Like Miss Goodwin, Mother was outstanding too, and went the second mile by a different route. Curiously, it began with the coal-oil can.

"Lloyd, I want you to take this can and go into town for some coal-oil. Go to Hearne's Hardware. Your dad and I have to go in for a few things, and we'll meet you at Eaton's at four o'clock. Off you go."

Although we lived on the edge of town, we had not yet graduated to a house with modern conveniences. Wood for the stove and oil for the lamps were still routine requirements. Getting in wood was not so bad. One could do that chore at home, out of sight of the sophisticated town mice. But going for coal-oil was a different matter. It led one right into the enemy camp, and exposed one to possible attack. And even if one tried to act like a town mouse, the coal-oil can was a dead giveaway. I went to town reluctantly.

The attack came on the brow of the last hill. As I passed the high hedge that surrounded the stately house on the corner, a bombardment of hawthorne berries rained down from over the hedge. Harmless missiles, their damage was more psychological than physical. Backed by a barrage of catcalls from the unseen gunners, the berries were effective enough to hasten me on my way.

"Back in town, hayseed?"

"Goin' for momma's coal oil, hayseed?"

"Goin' after roller skates, hayseed?"

"Beat it, hayseed."

I never did see the enemy, and lacked the courage to look. Hunkering down, and cursing the coal oil can, I beat it into town and sought out the hardware store.

I had wanted a bicycle as long as I could remember. My desire had increased with age and, even though my rambling had reduced it to a dream, I had convinced myself that the completion of the Entrance Exams might make it a reality. When I met my parents at Eaton's I thus entertained the thought that a bicycle might be the object of their trip to town. But after a few nonsensical purchases there, my parents talked endlessly with the store manager, Mr. Pickard, while I went outside to sulk.

On the way home, with me showing my disappointment by dragging behind them with the stupid coal oil, Mother suddenly stopped. "Alf, have you got that blue parcel from Eaton's?"

"No. I thought you had it."

"Well, I haven't. Lloyd, give me that coal oil and run along back to Eaton's. Go to Mr. Pickard, and ask him for our blue parcel. He'll know which one."

Back I went, cursing the forgetfulness and stupidity of all parents, and mine in particular. Seeking out Mr. Pickard, I asked for the stupid blue parcel. "My parents forgot it," I explained.

"Certainly, my boy. Come this way. It's at the back of the store."

I followed him past the Notions counter, through Men's Wear, and over to the Hardware Department.

"Ah, here it is," he exclaimed.

There it was indeed. The most beautiful, all-round jim-dandy blue C.C.M. bicycle one could imagine. Better by far than Sethie's old bike, superior even to Ken Darling's red one, this was brand-new, and had never been ridden, even once. With eyes glistening, I mumbled my thanks, and pushed the blue parcel out the door and onto the street.

My exaltation was momentarily dampened when I tried to ride down Main Street, only to find that the handlebars hadn't been tightened and the tires were flat. Both were remedied at the service station, however, and ten minutes later I caught up with the most thoughtful, most generous and intelligent parents in the world, walking along Brunel Road with the precious coal-oil can.

As I rode past, calling out my everlasting love and affection for them, my mother called after me.

"Remember. That bike goes back to Mr. Pickard if you fail them Entrance Exams."

A week later, I burst into the house to find Miss Goodwin there.

She'd never been there before, and my surprise overpowered my good manners.

"What are you doing here?" I asked.

"What am I doing here? Why, I'm here because the Entrance results are out."

"They are? Did I pass?"

"Did you pass? You did more than that. You won the gold medal!"

Poor Mother. Disarmed of her customary reserve, she sat there beaming as I blurted out "I did? You mean I even beat those town kids?"

"You certainly did. You even beat out those that didn't have to write, but were doing so only to win a medal. I'm really proud of you."

Successes were few and far between in my family's recent past, and I was not surprised when Mother said that she could hardly wait to tell Dad. When he came home that night, she greeted him with "The teacher was here today."

"She was? What'd she want?"

"Entrance results are out."

"Did he pass?"

She knew how much my father had counted on his son achieving at school. He rarely put his hopes into words, but she knew what it meant to him. Overcome by a moment of mischief, she answered with one word.

"No."

"He didn't? What marks did he get?" Dad seemed to shrink with her reply. Then, without the heart to continue the torture, Mother gave him the good news, and watched him hide his pleasure by blowing his nose.

"Son, I guess you get to keep that bike, after all. Thanks, son." And he blew his nose again.

Field Mouse Moves to Town

Becoming a town mouse was a defining experience for me. Of course, I already had "enjoyed" brief learning experiences in town; but they were like taking a swim; you went in, and you came back to dry land when you'd had enough. But actually moving into the lake—well, it was akin to becoming a fish!

Some of the changes were purely environmental; and although they provided new and even novel experiences on a day-to-day basis, they rarely touched my heart. But those that had a social context were the ones that reached in and gripped my very soul.

Of course, time had a lot to do with it. Had I been four or five, I would have scarcely noticed the move. And if I'd been twenty—why I'd have relished the adventure. But I was only thirteen, that difficult period of budding maturity when one is tentatively reaching out to find support and security among his fellows. It's the worst possible time to be transplanted—for a plant or a child. Farmers don't do it. But people often do, frequently because of circumstances beyond their control. So it was in my case. Because of "circumstances," I became a town mouse when I was most vulnerable.

History was also a factor. Today, technology and travel have diminished the differences between urban and rural life. But years ago, the divide was much greater. Not all country homes had electricity or indoor plumbing, and those two factors alone made for different worlds. Add streets and roads, electric power, indoor plumbing and a dash of main street hubris and you had the makings of a culture that was ready, willing, and able to set itself apart from the surrounding countryside. In fact, town and country had themselves been woven into a social fabric long before I came upon the scene. It was a fact of life stretching back almost to the beginning of civilization, and my brush with it was only made different from others by my moment in time. Myths and humour had long celebrated the ignorance of the "country bumpkin," and had become part of the national psyche by the time I arrived upon the scene. But the fact that it was well established did little to still my apprehension as I steeled myself to face the music.

Huntsville was a hive of industry and tourism when I came knocking. It had its rich and its poor, its gracious gentry and its abusive lords, just like many towns of the thirties. It was too large to get lost in and not too small to have only one side of the track. The answer to "Where do you live?" pretty well placed one in the social order. Even so, youth being what it is, one rarely found himself ostracized by class. The stigma of being a country mouse provided a much great burden than did the side of the tracks on which one lived.

My initiation into "urbanity" had an added feature. I lived on the edge of town, close enough to walk in, but far enough out to boast an outdoor toilet and oil lamps. I was neither "fish nor fowl" as they say. I was a town mouse by day and a field mouse by night.

But everyone knew my status. I was a boarder. My mother was a cook, either in a logging camp or Malloy's Restaurant. My dad was a worker, either in the camp or at the mill. And that's the way it was.

Heading for high school on that September morning in 1937, I experienced a fear akin to "going over the top" in World War I. With a pair of my brother's long pants cut down to size, and sporting a new shirt, sweater and haircut, I clutched my books, jumped on my bike that I got for passing my entrance exams, and rode off into the unknown. As it turned out, my bike suffered a worse fate than I. In the second week of my initiation as a town mouse, it was stolen from its place outside the school. "That guy from north Huntsville took it" was the rumour. But it was never found. I would have to continue the fight on foot.

The "enemies" weren't too bad, actually. They were much like the other kids I had known. As a matter of fact, I had brushed up against some of these same town mice during my brief but tortuous stop in their elementary class. And a boy named Harvey had shared earlier school adventures for four years in Ullswater. They sported a more up-scale, urban style of dress; and their cuss words were a little less earthbound; but after the ice was broken, I felt reasonably at home with these town mice. This comfort was considerably enhanced when, during a tussle with one of the enemy, a boy stepped in on my behalf—and became my friend for life. His name was Vern Payne.

"Anybody wants to take a poke at 'droopy drawers' here, will have to take me on first!" said Vern. He said it with such confidence and finality that my adversary backed off, and I accepted the sobriquet "droopy drawers" more with pleasure than with pain. It was true that my pants *did* droop a bit at the time, as did his. After all, we came from equal stations in life. Curiously, the term stuck, but only with him. He periodically addressed me thus over the next sixty years.

Without fanfare or announcement, Vern became our leader. He, too, was "from the other side of the tracks," and he had fourteen brothers and sisters to share his lot. He was accustomed to foraging for himself, and this gave him a sense of fortitude that set him apart from the rest of us.

Hugh Forsythe became a good friend, too. He enjoyed a more eminent position on the town's social scale, but it never got in the way as our friendship grew to extend beyond those testing days at school. Our skis tied us together. Mind you, his were more expensive than mine, and I admired his harness openly. But I had something special. I proudly sported my hand-made Finnish skis, complete with raw-hide harness, made for me a year earlier by that Finnish settler back in Ravensworth. They were the "Cadillac" of skis; and they went a long way in evening the balance between myself and the town skiers of Huntsville. Luckily, by the time I broke them a year later I felt sufficiently secure to take the loss philosophically. They had served their purpose.

As a boarder, I came and went from "no fixed address." "He lives out on the Brunel Road" was about as precise as it got. In fact, I boarded with Mrs. Evans, a dear old English lady in a little cabin in the bush just off the road. She was a widow who never tired of telling me how her husband fell off the sleigh when the teams ran away "and tore his guts right out!" She was a lovely landlady and constantly fretted over my welfare. Mother couldn't have chosen better. While I was with Mrs. Evans, Mother cooked at the logging camp at Bear Lake. Eager to see her, I caught a logging truck on its way to camp one Friday and spent a happy reunion overnight. When I left, she gave me seven dollars to pay Mrs. Evans for my board. And what did I do? Why, I bought a pair of second-hand skates—and made the hockey team as goaltender! Mrs. Evans would have to wait. Oh, she got paid later, and I paid later too, but that was a less glorious matter.

In the second year at school, fortune put the Dennis family in a rented house in the west end. It was brick and it had a twin next door. They hung precariously by the side of the cliff that faced the railway tracks, and they were so unattractive that I almost felt sorry for them. Our house was like a brick block, with two storeys and a stinking wee toilet in the cellar that was more demeaning than comfortable. "At least we won't have to go outside," said Mother. Looking at that toilet, I'd take the little house anytime!

I now had a place in town; and it was definitely on the wrong side of the tracks. Now in my second year in high school, and slowly gathering my self-esteem, I slipped a bit at the thought of inviting any of my friends here. As it turned out, only two ever crossed the threshold. That's right. Vern thought that I had "come up in the world," and Hugh enjoyed Mother's cooking so much that he left with only a culinary impression.

The house had some advantages. A steep hill reached down from the Catholic Church to the road, then continued past the house down to the tracks. It soon became my Olympic downhill. I would start at the top, sweep down across the road, jump the sidewalk and rush to the bottom, unscathed and triumphant. And of course, the house offered a short route to my brief but exciting job at the railway station where I loaded freight at three in the morning. More importantly, it gave my mother a base where she could make new friends. Not being a teenager, she found the conversion to the life in town less traumatic than I. Old or young, we had one thing in common: we both had friends.

I had something else, too. I parted with the money earned during the summer in favour of a brand new red bicycle—and a lock. It gave me a sense of control over my destiny, and I took every opportunity to use it to raise my station above the ordinary.

One Saturday, I wheeled down to the docks below the railway station and found a lone figure there, gazing idly out into Hunter's Bay. This was not unusual, since "Hobo Jungle" lay just beyond where the bridge spanned the river and in those days it was usually well occupied with the jobless transients, or "tramps" as they were sometimes called. "He is probably one of those," I thought. When I wheeled up to him, I was struck by the courteous urbanity with which he greeted me.

"Good afternoon young man," he said. "I was just admiring the beautiful panorama of nature that lies here within one's gaze. You are indeed fortunate to bask in such natural splendour"—or words to that effect.

I agreed with him, and after more one-sided chatter I determined that he was indeed, a tramp, and a hungry one at that. An idea jumped out at me.

"Just wait a minute. I'll be right back," I said.

Home I rode to raid the cupboard; and in no time at all, I had whipped up a cheese sandwich, a potato, and two of Mother's butter tarts. Gathering them into the bag, I jumped on my bike and was back. I handed him the bag. He looked inside, then looked at me and said "Thanks son. Years from now you will remember what you did for me today."

As I wheeled away I felt as if I had just moved to the other side of the tracks, somehow.

Teenage Workaholic

I grew up in a culture where the work ethic was more than a virtuous principle; it was a necessity for survival. As children, we grew into it through chores; and if a child found that there was nothing to do, he or she would not feel right, somehow. Even when play entered the day, there was always a tinge of guilt, an unconscious hope that at the end of the moment of freedom, a worthwhile task would present itself for the redemption of the sinner.

After I received my bike for passing my entrance exams, I got a job as a caddy at the Huntsville Downs, a golf course that lay about two miles north of town. Pedalling up the highway, I felt like the cyclists in E.T., leaving the surface of the road to enter a new world, devoted to pleasure and scenic beauty. Why, carrying a golf bag seemed only incidental in the major adventure of the day—to walk endlessly among the downs with no responsibility for how well the ball was played, or whether it was played at all!

In reality it was a little more arduous than that. The caddies would wait anxiously for a genial, generous customer, each hoping that he wouldn't be chosen by Mr. Sharpe, a local music teacher and organist who had a reputation for parsimony and playing with old balls. We got twenty-five cents for caddying nine holes, which included watching the ball when hit, finding it when lost, holding the pin, counting the strokes, and agreeing with the master should there be a difference in judgement. On a good day, we might make a whole dollar!

At noon, we would take turns rushing down to the nearby river for a skinny-dip; then it was back for another round. At the end of the day, Manager Ware would sometimes allow us to play a round with a three-iron, and some of us became as good as the players who were our masters. Of course, the search for lost balls was an unending habit. We were not allowed to sell them, but *could* turn them in at the clubhouse in exchange for a bottle of Orange Crush.

That drink came back to haunt me when I entered high school that fall. My good friend and "gang leader" Vern Payne worked after school at Mr. MacDonald's restaurant. One day he pressed three of us into going with him to Rotary Beach on Vernon Lake. The objective: to pick up crates of empty Orange Crush bottles left over from the summer season. So off we went in our Scoutmaster's borrowed 1932 Buick to pick up our load.

On the way home, Vern suddenly pulled the Buick over to the side of the road.

"Everybody out!" he ordered. Midst a chorus of questions about the need for this sudden halt, he explained. "We were told to pick up 'empty' cases. There's one full case among the empties. Everybody out! Start drinkin'."

And so it was that, on a hot September day in 1937, four young stalwarts knocked the caps off twenty-four bottles of warm Orange Crush, and consumed them all, then and there. After all, times were hard, and we couldn't let it go to waste!

I made reasonably good use of my spare time. I got a job at the railway station, which was not far from my house in the west end. I would jump out of bed each morning at two o'clock, rush down to the station, unlock the freight shed, lie down, and wait for the train that would arrive at three.

I felt a sense of budding maturity with this responsibility. There was a loaded .38 revolver in the desk drawer; and although no one had thought to instruct me as to its use, I got the impression that this was no ordinary job. I would lie there in the dark with a growing sense of importance and fear, until the sudden sound of the approaching train would jump-start me into action.

Throwing the shed doors open, I would pull the precious cargo to its appointed place on the platform and await the gaping door of the approaching car. It was a simple task, really. All one had to do was transfer the wagon's cargo to the waiting train, then return the wagon to the shed, lock up and go home.

But on my very first night I was reminded that it's the little things that count. There was a yellow line painted on the platform, beyond which it was unsafe to stand during train time. With my mind occupied by the importance of the moment, I failed to notice that the edge of the wagon's platform was pushing its luck. As the train crept by, its leading car scraped the wagon's corner, causing it to move ever so slightly. Certainly it was only a little thing; but it was big enough to warn me that only good fortune saved me from a disaster.

That task done, I raced back home to rest a bit before the next job beckoned. That was at the Post Office. My friend Vern already had a job there, and he had convinced Postmaster Mayhew that I would be worthy of employment as a mail sorter. I arrived each day at eight o'clock in the morning to face huge bins of mail waiting to be placed in rows of "pigeon holes" along the wall. I would pitch into the job, and just as I began to lose interest in the difference between 14 Portage Avenue and 114 Portage Road, Mr. Mayhew would tell me to get off to school. I found Miss Fenn's French class less challenging, somehow.

Suddenly, my career as a budding postmaster was over. Mr. Mayhew called me to his office one morning to announce that I was free to send mail all over the world as long as I didn't sort it in his post office. "Maybe it's because you're left handed," he said.

For me, the defining summer holidays job was at the Huntsville Trading Company, which stood on Main Street. Like a magnet, it attracted town and country folk alike. My friend Hugh worked in the men's department, but being more comfortable with meat and potatoes, I elected to work in the grocery store—which belied its real reach. It had a huge butcher shop, and sheds of flour and feed that would satisfy any farmer. Israel Ginsberg ran the Department store, while his brothers Abe and Morris operated the grocery world.

Each day when I arrived for work, I donned my white apron and jacket, and was suddenly transformed from a street kid into a young man of business—and the feeling was quite remarkable. Encouraged by the firm but amiable Abe Ginsberg, I so absorbed myself in the world of work that I was almost disappointed at the end of the day.

"Sugar madam? Certainly. How many pounds. And raisins? Yes, two pounds coming right away." Then it was out to the feed shed to get that farmer two bags of chop and a bag of oats. I even helped out in the butcher shop, upon occasion; and when I carelessly cut my hand there, Mr. Ginsberg took me to the doctor without a word of admonishment. One could safely say that by the end of the first two weeks of summer, I had learned a good deal about the retail trade.

On two occasions they allowed me to deliver feed with their small truck. The first was a local run, just to the edge of town. But the second was beyond Utterson, a distance of about ten miles. With a budding sense of adulthood, I asked my girlfriend to go along. From "the other side of the tracks," she probably felt that it was time to see how my side lived, and agreed to come. It was a safe trip—for her, for the truck and for the two bags of feed. As for me, it was one step closer to becoming a man of the world. Mind you, when my love's mother visited the butcher shop, I headed for the cellar. I suspected that she would see nothing "worldly" in my waiting upon customers in a grocery store.

Saturday was always a long day. It began before the store opened when we unloaded the fruit from the truck and arranged the baskets along the storefront. When the doors opened, the people would swarm the store like bees, and we'd be kept running to meet their many demands. On into the night it went, and just as I felt like dropping dead, the call would come to "get those baskets off the street!" Load after load we carried, until the last forlorn six-quart basket of grapes was safely inside the store. Only then could I surrender my uniform of business and head for home, lucky to be alive.

At the end of one day, Morris Ginsberg found my till short by six cents. He kindly admonished me, and I promised to make it up. But since I had already sensed his good humour, I decided to mail it to him, "postage due." I was right. He could hardly contain himself when my father entered the store shortly thereafter and was met with "You've got one bright young businessman there, Mr. Dennis! He owes me six cents, and what does he do? He mails it to me postage due! He'll go far, just wait and see!" And they laughed together.

They laughed together. This was especially significant to me. The Dennis family had done business with the brothers before, and their relationship had always been respectful and friendly. They respected and liked them. But the eviction from Ullswater still hurt, respect and friendship aside.

In my last summer there, I noticed that a small, foreign-speaking boy had joined our staff. He was eager to work and unerringly courteous, and I finally surmised that he was an escapee from the boiling pot that the Jewish people had encountered in Europe. Though I had only a teenage awareness of this horror that Hitler had produced, I knew enough to admire the Ginsbergs for what they apparently had done. Only after the war did I learn of the extent of the holocaust, and the shameful role that our country played in failing to reach out as a nation to help the helpless. That was left to individuals like the Ginsbergs, who doubtless did what they could against great odds.

Ecclestone's Hardware beckoned me during my last summer at the grocery store, and offered to pay me a dollar more per week. My mother came to see Mr. Ginsberg about it, and I can still remember his encouraging reply:

"Lloyd is a good young worker, Mrs. Dennis, and you are a nice family. Let him stay with me and I promise you should he ever need any help in the future, tell him to come and see me."

Although that promise was never fulfilled when opportunity knocked years later, his complimentary remarks to my mother were help enough. I stayed.

Tasty Treasures

Mother called me a "picky eater." And given her reputation as a formidable cook, I don't suppose that my selective approach to food won me points at the table. I began life by shunning milk. The story goes that I broke my first bottle and became a "teetotaler" thereafter, as far as milk was concerned. Warm sweet tea became my beverage of choice. Porridge joined the rejection list, as did all vegetables other than potatoes, corn and peas. Mind you, Mother managed to sneak the unwanted into my gullet by hiding them in the midst of something irresistible, like beef stew or chicken pot pie; but alone and unaided, they stood a slim chance of finding their way to my stomach. I'd rather do without—which often was the case.

I wasn't a big eater anyway, so I never felt deprived. Dad was of similar disposition. He worked hard, but I never saw him eat with gusto; and although he wasn't particular in his choice of food, he ate sparingly, as if his small frame could not carry the burden of bountiful food.

Mother and my brother Vernon were cut from a different mould. Large and robust, their plates carried the weight for Dad and me. But other than the odd jibe such as "You two don't eat enough to keep a bird alive," Mother regularly mounted the table with whatever was available; and poor as we often were, there always seemed to be plenty to eat. The old adage "clean your plate" was a common admonition of the day, and in that regard, Dad and I got off lightly. We were careful not to put too much there in the first place.

I was a more rabid fan of Mother's culinary skills in the dessert department. She told everyone who cared to listen that I had a "sweet tooth," while avoiding any responsibility for my predilection with that part of her output. Her butterscotch pies were the talk of the Ladies Aid—and of any other group fortunate enough to partake of them. Other pies were equally delicious, from strawberry and rhubarb, to raisin, lemon and apple. Also heralded were her breads, her biscuits and rolls, the most famous of which were the Parker House, a particular favourite of tourists who cottaged at Simolean Beach in Ullswater. A lifetime later, I tried to re-create them in my own kitchen; but they were a very pale image of what my mother's magic used to create. And once, while she visited me, I asked her to direct me step by step in the re-creation of her beautiful butterscotch pie. I slavishly did as I was told, only to stand defeated by the result. "At least it's the same colour," she consoled.

Many other delights spewed in abundance from her oven. Oatmeal, chocolate and ice-box cookies vied for first place with her "snowballs," which were really chocolate clumps rolled in coconut. She had a special touch with shortbread, perhaps aided by rice flour. Her butter tarts were exquisite and her Christmas fruit cake with almond icing is still lodged in my memory, along with her delicious layered chocolate cake which was reputedly made more delectable by the presence of mayonnaise. And, should my sweet tooth require treatment by a more down-to-earth brand of sweet, she would whip up chocolate fudge with the best of them.

My earliest encounters with manufactured confectionary occurred at Brown's store in Martin's Siding, Janet McNicoll's store in Allensville, and Clarke's General Store in Utterson. One of the first to force itself upon me was a paper tube of popcorn, worth one cent. It shared shelf space with large jars filled with peppermints, "pattercrisp" pieces, jelly beans, rock candy, licorice, maple buds and other delights whose names I can't remember. Apart from its odd tubular shape, the popcorn didn't have that much going for it. But what really captured my interest—and my taste buds—was the licorice. It offered itself in the form of little pipes and pieces shaped like small plugs of tobacco. The plugs sported a tiny round shield emblazoned with an Indian head, and the pipe's crown was studded with tiny red beads of candy. Like the popcorn, each could be mine for one cent. I can taste them yet.

There were personal habits of eating that both my mother and I had acquired by the time I was about twelve. They were never discussed, or even mentioned; but they were there, nonetheless, and when my memory drifts toward Mother's kitchen, they jump out with the rest. One wasn't a food. It was a medicine Mother always took daily. Not only did she consume aspirin pills, she did so with relish. I found them fit only for a quick swallow, to be followed by water. But Mother? Why, she would toss them into her mouth and chew them as if they were candy. She did it when I was young, and she was still at it before she died in her ninetieth year. It was the common aspirin tablet.

Her other "habit" was slightly more attractive. She always seemed to have an apron pocket full of rolled oats, ready for constant consumption. She was unobtrusive about it, and to her it was no big thing. And after a while, I copied the habit, and went to school with at least one pocket full of rolled oats. Later on, she shifted to peanuts for a time—and so did I. One day I got a rude surprise that is still in my treasure chest of memories. I was in Falkenburg school at the time, and in the habit of pilfering the odd tiny piece of chalk from the ledge of the blackboard. Home I headed one fine fall day with the chalk in my pocket, along with a handful of peanuts. Well, the reader can guess the rest. I wandered in to greet Mother, and idly asked her if she noticed anything different about her mouthful of peanuts, which she was munching at the time. "No," she replied, "But you seem to be having trouble. What do you know that I don't?" When I spat out the gooey mess of mush, I remembered the chalk—and swore off both for at least a week.

By the time I reached high school, I had developed a new habit. While working at the Huntsville Trading Company, I began tossing wheat into my mouth, which was available in great abundance out in the feed shed. It ground up well, and had a taste more in keeping with my teenage status. Before long, I was "addicted" to it, and even kept a bowl by my bed at night! I carried it to school, to the show, and wherever else I went. I ate it furtively, almost as if it were an illegal substance, and felt somehow unarmed if I were without it. So Mother munched her oatmeal, and I chewed my wheat, and if the world noticed, it didn't let on.

It was about that time that I picked up another habit—eating raw potatoes. Whether the wheat supply ran out or I tired of the effort, I can't remember. I only recall going to school, regularly supplied with a washed but unpeeled potato always in my pocket, ready to be devoured whenever hunger called. I became quite enamored of the taste; and since potatoes were a staple in our house, the supply was endless—and cheap. How fortunate it was for my parents that my tastes didn't run to more expensive treasures!

The winds of fortune blew cold for the Dennis family during the Depression years. But few could say that they were better fed than we were. Thanks to the ingenuity and hard work of my mother, our palates tasted delights arguably unmatched by fancier fare. Add regular dashes of oatmeal, a few handfuls of wheat and the odd raw potato—and what more could one ask to provide a tasty treasure?

Up, Out and Away

In Europe, the clouds of war shut out the sun on that day in 1939. But in Huntsville, that sun was free to bathe the townsfolk with an autumn warmth that is a trademark of Muskoka. It lit the gold of the maple hills, touched the red roof of the Lookout, and reflected the blue sky in the river winding through the town. One of its rays fell upon the east windows of the Huntsville High School. It caught the eye of Vern, erstwhile leader of the Gang, and for the moment, an easily distracted student in Miss Gibbs' Latin class.

To understand what happened then, one has to appreciate that for Muskoka, the autumn sun does more than offer warmth and light. It casts a spell. Those who have felt its September rays in that part of the world will tell you that the sun is almost magnetic as it beckons one to follow it to the open air. It touches the skies, lights the eye, and fills its victim with strange thoughts of freedom from the ordinary toil of daily life. Its power has no respect for age, and reaches out to old and young alike; and although adults are generally more practical in resisting the call of the autumn sun, the young are especially susceptible, and find it virtually impossible to do anything purposeful under the sun.

Vern was no exception. In fact, at that moment he was a particularly good example of sun-struck youth. Thoughts of sun-drenched country roads, the blue waters, and the fall marshes that all lay just beyond the town, danced through his mind. The smell of the fall dilated his nose in imagination, and made the smell of chalk-dust in the room seem especially repugnant. Added to this was his admitted disinterest in Hannibal scaling the Alps—especially in a tongue not only foreign but dead to boot. The mixture of such alien ingredients as those offered by Muskoka's autumn and Miss Gibbs' Latin class was too much. As the teacher turned to write on the blackboard, Vern reached for the window and quietly raised it.

Every member of the Gang saw the window open upon the world. In fact, each had been similarly smitten by fall (although it was tacitly agreed that the most intense feeling was reserved for the leader). Hugh, Lyle, Mac and Lloyd, almost with one accord, looked expectantly to that leader for some sign of command. It was not long in coming. Long before Miss Gibbs reached the end of her sentence, they had followed their leader to the window, and one at a time and ever so silently, they were up, out and away.

This account won't dwell upon the details of that adventure. Needless to say, it was the work of the sun upon the hopeless young souls who found their feet carrying them like wings, far from Hannibal, Miss Gibbs, and everything scholarly that good old Huntsville

High School had to offer. Obviously, they had each answered a call that was beyond human understanding. In fact, the group had gone some distance before one of its members found it necessary to ask, "Where are we going?"

"Duck hunting," came the terse reply.

It was shortly after nine the next morning that the Gang, with their spirits now satiated by the previous day's adventure, found themselves called to the office of the principal. The moment had come. Soon the world would know if the pull of the autumn sun was powerful enough even to affect the mind of a high school principal. Each young hunter stood, and with various affectations of savage courage, sauntered on his way to glory.

Modern-day learners won't know of the principal's office in old Huntsville High School. It hung halfway between the first and second floors, a partitioned part of the stairway landing that served as a sort of "point of passage" for both up and down traffic. Its doorway was a convenient vantage point for the principal who, at the time of this event, was Mr. Harry Thornton. There he would stand, ready, willing and able to greet the young flow of Huntsville humanity—and to summon those whose actions were in need of punishment or praise. Not so large as a modern school's broom closet, it nevertheless was the scene of judgement for many a young hopeful, caught in the vicissitudes of growing up in high school. It was soon called upon for just such a scene.

Mr. Thornton's greeting was unexpectedly kindly. In fact, his opening comments about the fall and its captivating weather were so benign and inviting that in no time at all the boys found themselves almost eager to share their beautiful experience of the hunt with him. With growing enthusiasm they added detail upon detail, led on by his enthusiastic queries. It all seemed so natural. After all, why *wouldn't* another man be a kindred spirit? Distance between man and boy, between principal and student, fell away in the telling of that brief escape from daily toil at school.

Suddenly, the beautiful spirit of camaraderie came to an end. With a slap of his desk, Mr. Thornton returned to the rarified world of the school principal, and drawing himself up to a height roughly estimated at fourteen feet, levelled a blast at the five young hunters that rings in the ears of the author to this day. With gathering force, he outlined the trials of principalship fraught as it was with hunters instead of scholars. As flecks of foam formed on his lips, and as the very chalk-dust fled from his suit, he laboured over his point of justice wherein he, as a great lover of the Autumn himself, was nevertheless forced by duty to remain in his school, the guardian of our welfare—which at the moment seemed to us to be in great jeopardy. At this rate, each of us assumed, his rage would lead at least to expulsion. Perhaps we were about to be exiled to a period of duck hunting that would last till Thanksgiving—or beyond!

It was not to be. As suddenly as the storm arose, it died. Perhaps he sensed that exile would mean even more hunting and less learning. Perhaps he saw the futility of joining Hannibal in combatting the Autumn spell which captured us. Perhaps because he saw himself in us, a kindred spirit, different only in time and duty. Whatever the reason, he stopped the onslaught.

"Get back to your class," he said. "And if I ever so much as suspect that you are planning such a caper again, I'll go hunting myself—and you will be five dead ducks!"

Years and years later, I stood as a teacher one fine fall day and recalled that long ago incident in Huntsville High School. Suddenly I found myself telling the class of our exploit. How the sun had beckoned, and we had jumped out the window to go hunting. The class, in historical tradition, listened appreciatively as their teacher dipped back into his boyhood to tell of his old school days. Only by great exertion was I able to pull myself out of my past and return the class to more meaningful things which at that moment, were prescribed as history. In any case, we left Huntsville and the Gang's duck hunt and returned to the study of a more noteworthy past. Some time later, my principal knocked at my classroom door. "Are you missing any pupils?" he asked.

I quickly scanned the five rows of captive historians. Sure enough, big Bob Lane was not in his usual place, last seat in the window row. Before I had time to answer, the principal answered for me. "You needn't tell me," he said. "The whole world probably knows by now. One of our interested tax-payers was passing the school, and there, right before his eyes, was a student, removing himself from your class by means of that open window. I don't know what you intend to do about it, but I'll tell you one thing. If another student leaves your class by that route and I find out about it, I suggest that you follow him."

Alas, I didn't have it in me to tell him that I had already used such an exit years ago, and that the present city miscreant was but a faithful follower of the example that had been set so long ago in my old alma mater, Huntsville High School.

Canadians! Canadians! That's All!

Scarcely twenty years had passed since the greatest war in history had ended. Yet, to the young bloods of Huntsville High School, one scarcely gave thought to that great tragedy. True, the tattered remnants of Canada's contribution lay scattered like leaves across the countryside; but Canadian youth rarely gave them a second thought. Over 800,000 Canadians saw service for the "Mother Country," and more than 60,000 of them fell in battle. But Canadians, young and old, behaved almost as if nothing had happened. Times were hard; but they were even harder for many of the veterans who, often crippled, shell-shocked or poisoned by gas, had to struggle for a living in the midst of a depression and a seemingly ungrateful public.

My Uncle Henry was one of them. He was a quiet, defeated man, permanently affected by the enemy gas attack near Ypres. And I can still remember him patiently answering my silly questions such as "Did you use a bow and arrow in the war?" I was only about seven or eight at the time, but as I recall, I was the only one who seemed interested in what he had suffered. My friend Hugh's father was a veteran, too. He could proudly say that not only had he been through the war, he had been there at the end, to witness the triumph at Mons, a city from which the British had retreated four years earlier. These men were only two of the many who had gone to war from the district. But there were many more, now almost invisible in the public struggle for a more fortunate time.

A few things kept their glory alive, public indifference notwithstanding. Our school readers were sprinkled with the glories of the Empire, inspired by victories in the Crimea, South Africa, Canada and Europe. A few records of war songs could be heard across the land, plaintively reminding everyone that it was a long way to Tipperary, and that marching to Pretoria was once a thing to do in South Africa. And as for Mademoiselle from Armentiéres, well, enough said!

One tale that caught my eye was in the fourth reader, the year before high school. Called "Canadians! Canadians! That's All!", it was taken from a book called *Private Peat*, written by veteran Harold Peat, and tells of an heroic incident in April 1915 where the Canadians held the line at St. Julien, near Ypres. Because they stood fast, their British comrades were able to link up with them; and it was their cry of praise that gave rise to the title of the story.

The capture of Vimy Ridge was another heroic Canadian moment, where on April 9, 1917, our troops took the ridge after several failed attempts by other forces. Some say that it was our defining moment as a nation. So notable was the feat that a stunning memorial was erected there, and introduced to the public by His Majesty King Edward VIII in 1936. That caught our attention, for a moment, at least. What a pity that, despite numerous requests made almost a century later, the British still refuse to return our flag carried at that battle from its place in the Imperial War Museum. Ah, well.

I hadn't needed a memorial to awaken my interest in war. The flame was lit as early as 1934, when a newspaper printed a whole page of gory pictures of death on the western front. One picture still appears in my mind. It showed a virtual skeleton of a soldier hanging on the barbed wire that stretched in front of the trench. It fanned the flame lit by Uncle Henry, and got such noisy assistance from old gramophone records that soon I was marching around the parlour like a real soldier. And I can still remember my mother singing, "Oh tell us all about the war, and what we fought each other for."

But now I was in high school, becoming increasingly indifferent even to the reminder of the local Royal Canadian Legion that the Huntsville area had lost twenty-one men to the Great War. Colonel Lawlor, a famous local hero of war, came to talk to us at school. But what he said was lost in the busy teenage affairs of the moment. After all, there were many more important things going on. Games and girls topped the list, followed in turn by skiing, skating, hunting and fishing—to say nothing of the struggle to become a proper town mouse.

Then it happened. The radio bleated bleakly with the news of impending war. The paper ran stories of a strutting, shouting character called Adolf Hitler, and out of nowhere, a scrawny foreign kid appeared beside me when I worked at the Ginsberg brothers' store. Doubtless plucked from the jaws of death in Europe, he was endlessly eager to help, and I asked no questions. The usually benign conversations on Saturday night street corners gave way to more strident gossip about real and imagined events that were taking place.

"They'll not get my boys!" one mother was heard to say. "Look what the last war did to my Bill—and his brother Harry!"

"My son can hardly wait," was the rejoinder. "He says that if war comes, he's goin' to join the air force."

One day, reserves of the Algonquin Regiment marched through town, all the way from Bracebridge! The hair on my neck bristled as I watched the long line of soldiers winding its way down Main Street, resplendent in the uniform of the Great War. Talk about being ready! They broke off their march momentarily, and I met my cousin Reg from Bracebridge among the men that drifted into Selrite's store. He seemed all grown up, in his tight jacket and long puttees. Then, on another fine day in 1939, principal Harry Thornton gathered us all in the fifth-floor room where we met silently while the malevolent ranting of Herr Hitler blasted us cold from the school's only radio. It had come at last. Now we wouldn't have to listen to endless tales of a war that happened before we were even born. We would have one of our own! The only question was, would it last long enough for us to get into it?

The war, of course, was about to begin half a world away from Huntsville. But already it reached out with its evil claws to scratch our town. Rumour had it that good old Mr. Massey, our revered teacher and coach, was probably a Hitler lover! Why else would he have gone to study in Germany? And what about that Brenner guy? He's German, isn't he? Better be careful what you say around him! Let's see. What other Germans have we got around town? Hans Brenner was a boy who played his violin with me in Sunday school. Finally, he dropped out, and I never saw him again. Were he and his father among the war's first victims? I'll never know.

A recruitment billboard appeared in town. It showed a blond young pilot, complete with flowing white scarf, carrying the message "You, too, can join the Royal Canadian Air Force." We could hardly wait. One day I began to see my friend Vern's older brother appear regularly at the back of the room after class. Howard Payne had already left school, but returned to have his mathematics skills revived by Mr. Thornton. Why? you ask. Because Howard saw the billboard, and was on his way to glory. Then, one after the other, young men of the town disappeared—and we knew why. If only it would last till our turn came.

One by one, those turns did come. And when it was all over, thirty-two never returned.

Howard Payne? He did, indeed, become a pilot, but he crashed on January 9, 1942. And now he lies with dozens of other fliers in a quiet cemetery in Skopwick, England. Right next to him is John Gillespie Magee, the author of *High Flight*. He had died only three weeks earlier. Perhaps they knew each other.

Play Up! Play Up! Play the Game!

For most rural youngsters, sports consisted of primitive activities borne of a primeval urge to burn off the excess energy of youth. They often consisted of racing along the road with hoops and sticks, playing fox and hound at noon-hour, or skinny-dipping in the nearby lake. Oh, I remember the odd attempt to play softball at nearby Bent River and Utterson; and I even recall playing rudimentary hockey on the winter roads, using frozen "horse buns" as pucks. But these forays were far removed from the athletic challenges that presented themselves at high school.

Man first landed on the moon in 1969. But I'm certain that I preempted their experience more than thirty years earlier when I entered high school in 1937. Beyond the social world of the town mice already described was a virtual colosseum of young gladiators ready, willing and able to form teams and take on the whole world. A makeshift gym beckoned to us from its place in the basement, complete with jumping horse, nets and bars. Outside lay a primitive area for softball and soccer, on call for our competent coach and Science teacher, Mr. Massey. And as if that weren't enough, an honest-to-goodness arena stood seductively on the edge of the fairgrounds, and outdoor rinks were on both ends of town! It was almost enough to make a kid from the sticks wet his pants just to look at it all.

Of course, Huntsville was no slouch when it came to sports. It long had teams competing in hockey, lacrosse and baseball, and was an early site for cricket matches late in the nineteenth century. Already there were "stars" of note in the town, which could also lay claim to three athletes of Olympic proportion. Abbott Conway and Larry O'Connor were both on Canada's track and field team, which went to the 1936 Olympics in Germany, and both represented Canada in the British Empire Games held in Australia in 1938. Hattie Briggs gained fame at the Lake Placid Olympics in 1933, where she won a silver medal in speed-skating, and was on the Canadian team at the 1936 Olympics in Germany.

And Jack Bionda? Well, he was just a kid at the time I joined the town mice. But he would go on to earn fame in lacrosse *and* hockey. No wonder the present arena is named for him!

There were plenty of fine examples for young stalwarts like me to emulate.

But it wasn't enough to play at home. We had to take on other towns! In no time at all I found myself on a track and field team, competing in Gravenhurst. I'm certain that I was an unremarkable competitor, but my claim to fame, at least privately, was to be chosen as speaker at the homecoming dinner held at the local Presbyterian Church, where I uttered the immortal words. "We won the Meet—and brought home the bacon!" It was the first bon mot of my public life, and I earnestly hoped that my town mice colleagues appreciated my new-found wit!

Soccer was given extra oxygen due to the fact that coach Norman Massey had studied in Heidelberg, Germany, and doubtless had fired his enthusiasm there, where "foosball" was—and is—the prime national sport. If Mr. Massey found us a disappointing reflection of his German experience, he never let on, and gave serious attention to the development of our skills. Poor man! He faced a double challenge. Not only were his recruits as green as cucumbers, the slope of the school's yard denied all and sundry a level playing field that even foreign experience couldn't overcome. We played anyway; and the game added a precious ingredient to the urban conversion that I was experiencing.

Although I was being accepted in town more readily than anticipated, such was not the case for one poor lad. He had recently come from Greece, and his language loudly labelled him as an "outsider." But when he hit that soccer field, his superior skill won all hearts over. Almost instantly, the town had claimed him as one of their own. And it remained that way, even after the soccer season was over.

Lacrosse had been a Huntsville game almost since the town's inception, and our Blackhawks made Huntsville "one of the best lacrosse towns in Ontario." And guess who was the leading scorer when they won the Eastern Canadian Championship? Why, Jack Bionda, of course! When we organized a lacrosse team, I elected to play goal; and armed with pads and the appropriate stick, I soon discovered a new description for self-destruction. But I stuck with it, and took another step on my long road to adulthood.

Hockey had its own champions. Its first OHA team was the Maroons, and its players provided ample examples for our school team. Having just purchased my first skates with my board money, I was, to say the least, a weak link in the chain. But I'd already survived as goalie in lacrosse, so it seemed reasonable that I should play goal in hockey. And I can still remember that heady feeling of nervous excitement as I played my first game in Huntsville's arena. There were actually people watching, even cheering us on! If anyone needed a reason to do well, that was it. To see my friend Vern playing defence helped immensely. In my mind, he could stop anybody! And my other pal, Hugh—why he was such an able forward that the enemy might never get to me!

But they often did; and I remember playing one night when a well-aimed puck made a defining mark on my life. We were playing for the Slater Cup, and had already defeated Milford Bay and Bracebridge. Now we were in Gravenhurst, intent upon claiming victory. It was the third period of a tightly fought game, with Huntsville leading by one goal when, *bam*, the puck caught me between the legs, and since I wasn't wearing an athletic support, I was suddenly where you'd expect—flat on the ice, writhing in pain.

What increased the pain tenfold was the fact that my girlfriend was in the stands, and since our very proper relationship would not even admit that I was so humanly endowed, I knew that my prostration on the ice could never be properly explained. Finally, dazed and embarrassed, I struggled to my feet. And where was the puck? Lying on the ice *outside* the line!

Ten minutes later, the game was over. The Slater Cup was formally presented to our captain, and we rode home, triumphant. My girlfriend never did ask what drove me to the ice, and I never told her. Let sleeping dogs lie, my mother used to say.

Everything has its season. Spring found us in the park, warming up for softball. We were a motley crew who bore a strong resemblance to our hockey and lacrosse teams. Bereft of a goal to tend, I played short-stop or right field. And memory tells me that I even pitched a game or two. It doesn't matter. What I do remember is our team winning the silver medal and I even have a picture to prove it. Then a bigger game started in Europe. It was much larger and far more deadly. Before it ended, it had recruited most of the players of good old Huntsville High School, and some never came back.

A Budding Man of the Cloth

God entered my life by the back door, you might say. I know that my parents took me to the church in Aspdin, the village in which I was born—and you may even have seen that tiny house of worship if you saw the original *Incredible Journey*. It's the little white building sliding past on the left of the screen as the plane sweeps by in the opening shot. I remember the flies on the windowpanes, and trying to count them as the preacher droned on. I remember the drive-shed where the men gathered to gossip around their horses and buggies. In Martin's Siding, I even went to Sunday school for a time and was proud of the few attendance cards which I collected. And in Ullswater, we made frequent long walks to the Anglican Church where I first heard my dad sing. He was good, too. It was only later that I learned that he had been a choirboy in Leeds, England, and had even sung in Paris.

In Utterson, I remember the precious visits by the same minister whom I had met at Aspdin, Reverend Laycock. He would drop in for tea with my mother when he came to preach there. I even got a lasting message from him during one of those visits. When Mother scolded me for having mud on my boots, he said, "Never mind, Lloyd, it's only clean dirt you have there." I guess God knew the difference.

But I really got close to Heaven through funerals. First, it was Mother's father who died in Allensville while we youngsters played out in the sandbank. Then it was Grandma's turn; and I still remember the hymns they sang at her funeral—which was held in a house. "Rock of Ages" and "Abide with Me" were steps on my musical road to going straight! These were followed by a number of aunts and uncles who died over the years of my childhood; so one could say that by the time I got to Huntsville, I knew which way the game was to be played. You played by the rules, if you knew what was good for you; and at an early age I had a pretty dramatic idea of what lay in store for the good *and* the bad. It might turn out to be just that—only an idea. But I chose to play it safe, just in case.

We joined the United Church in Huntsville, and got to meet the new minister. He was a beautiful human being, Reverend Beverley Oaten. He radiated like the sun, and greeted my parents like sheep lost from the flock. In no time at all, I had joined my friend Hugh Forsythe in Sunday school, the church choir, and the boys' group called Tuxis. Why, I felt closer to Heaven already—and I wasn't even sick! It was a giant step on the road to adulthood, and my cup of satisfaction was filling to the brim.

I lost a little when I left my fedora in the church after service one day; and the loss hurt more when my friend Vern opined that if I'd left it in *his* church, it would have been there when I went back to get it. Vern was an indifferent Anglican. No matter. The fedora was gone, and I never had another.

That choir was something else. Hugh and I were put in second bass; and what we lacked in tone was made up in giggling. The problem was, we sat beside Roy Skinner, a man of unknown age whose prime purpose seemed to be whispering jokes to us that were outrageous—and funny. Until that time in my life, I had never, ever, had my self-control tested so severely. Nor had Hugh. And the tougher it got, the more he tested us. Even the impassioned minister, engrossed as he was with his flock, would sometimes briefly turn as if to say, "Why in hell don't you shut up and at least *look* like you are listening!" And just when we were about to wet ourselves with the agony of suppressed humour, we would all stand, and Roy, of all people, would belt out "Jerusalem" as if he were God himself! It was a transcending experience, fundamental in the transformation of this particular country mouse. Adding spice to the event was the fact that we, black robed and majestic, faced the congregation, and our every twitch was there for all to see. As it was a mixed choir, a saving grace for me was the fact that the ladies sat on tiers below us. Thus my flame of the moment was unable to see me in my hilarious discomfort. For all she knew, I was the one who bellowed out "Jerusalem!" She was in the C.G.I.T., a girls' church group roughly equivalent to our Tuxis band. It stood for "Canadian Girls In Training," but I never did learn for what they were training. Events were moving too quickly in another direction.

There was a Boys' Work Board in Ontario at the time. This organization, among other good works, provided a novel annual experience for youth of the church. Every year during the Christmas break, they set up a mock parliament and situated it on the campus of McMaster University in Hamilton. Called The Older Boys' Parliament, it drew from constituents of the United Church all over Ontario. And those fortunate enough to go spent a week in sessions that had all the trimmings of the "real thing" in Ottawa. Members deliberated moral issues of the day, like alcohol abuse, depraved behaviour, cheating, theft and all such weaknesses of the human spirit. Bob Boyer, later the MPP for Muskoka, had once attended, and that added a touch of class to the whole thing.

Reverend Oaten had an idea. Why not have a contest for the Tuxis group? It could be built around Canadian artists, and, since Tom Thomson had once been a familiar face in town, it could lean heavily upon the Group of Seven. The proposal excited me. I may not have been the best sport in the world, but I liked art. I entered the fray with uncommon interest, and when the results were announced, I was declared the winner. "Lloyd Dennis will be Muskoka's next member of Older Boys' Parliament for 1939," announced Reverend Oaten, and my friend Hugh was the first to pump my hand. "When you get to parliament," he said, "you could use that presentation that won you the medal at the Canadian Women's Temperance Union," he suggested.

Thus it was that, the day after Boxing Day, resplendent in a jacket borrowed from a friend of my brother, I caught the train for Hamilton. The university was out of this world. Built of imposing grey stone and dressed with laced leaded windows, it was like a castle to me, the finest building I had ever seen. And the feeling of being in another world sharpened as I began to mix with my fellow Ontarians. They were from all over, from Timmins to Toronto, and were at least seventy in number. Doubtless, most of them felt as self-conscious as I, and I secretly wondered how many were wearing jackets not their own.

Borrowed or not, those jackets were soon bonded together in neat rows of parliament, as we took turns arguing the issues of the day. When called by the Speaker of the House, I made my maiden speech which, as Hugh had suggested, carried a severe admonition to beware the evil of drink—and all other sins. I sat down, wondering if my words had changed the world.

A number of my new-found friends went on to become public figures in Ontario life, and I crossed paths with several of them as time went on.

I came home enlightened in one unexpected regard. I had met the first black man of my life. His name was Wilbur Howard, a genial senior youth who impressed me greatly. He was one of the leaders of the Assembly, and fate would decree that he was well chosen. He went on to become a Moderator of the United Church of Canada.

When I returned home, Reverend Oaten was quick to present his "member of parliament" to a number of congregations in Muskoka; and I well remember the winter drives to places like Bala and Bracebridge. But it was Huntsville that became the summit of my success. Dad wouldn't be there, of course. He was working as bookkeeper and caretaker of Tynoka Lodge, out on Rebecca Lake. But my mother and brother would be there. So would Hugh and my other friends. Even Vern might come and, of course, as faithful church-goers, SHE and her family would be in their accustomed place.

I looked down from the exalted height of the pulpit. There was my family in the rear pew—but who was that? Why, it was Dad! Somehow he had managed to overcome the winter distance from Rebecca Lake and be present at his son's inaugural public presentation. And there he was loudly adorned—in a red shirt! My pulse quickened as I looked at the congregation, expecting them to turn as one and say, "That man in the red shirt! Why, that's Lloyd's father! Do you suppose that he is drunk?"

No, my father wasn't drunk. Nor could be. He was a teetotaler. But he'd had a burning desire to see his son where he himself might have been if life's cards had been dealt differently. And even that night Fate dealt to him another bad card. While he was in church, feeling proud of his son, Tynoka was set on fire by an angry employee. Dad, of course, lost his job.

But he always said that my speech was worth it.

Mother Always Called It a Fiddle

For my family, the "dirty thirties," as the Depression was called, meant more than a struggle for survival. It was also a battle for respectability. Our parents had never been wealthy. But as a young couple, they weren't down and out, either. Each had a strong desire to form a "respectable" family, to raise their children to do the "right" thing. "It don't cost nothin' to do the right thing," my mother would say, with utter disregard for the King's English. And if she felt that we could afford it, doing the "proper" thing would be even better. She disdained those who put on airs, but she yearned for a better life for us all and, along with Dad, did her level best to capture some symbol of success, however elusive it might be.

I think that this search is what led her in 1937 to surprise me with a gift. It cost all of seven dollars, and came in the shape of a red violin, complete with bow, resin and case. She pushed aside the fact that I was left-handed, had never indicated a thirst to play, and would probably end up as yet another disappointment for her. I accepted it with half-hearted thanks, and tried to feel grateful to the unknown horses who had sacrificed their tails for the bow.

I was no stranger to the instrument, of course. Although I had never owned one, the music of the fiddle was a regular and welcome visitor to my ears. As long as I could remember, my parents went to square dances in whatever community we lived; and I was one of the regulars among the children who "behaved themselves" on the sidelines while their parents swung with abandon to the tunes "Turkey in the Straw," "Soldier's Joy" or some such jig of the times. Without my knowing it, the instrument had sawn its way into my soul, so that at the time of its arrival on my doorstep I was, almost subconsciously, one of its fans. But the idea of actually playing it had never occurred to me.

"Now you take care of that fiddle, you hear?" she admonished. "Once you learn to play it, you might even end up in some concert, and we'll get to come and listen along with the rest of 'em." The "rest of 'em" no doubt would include people from the "other side of the tracks"; and perhaps she saw my playing as the ultimate opportunity to join them on equal terms, however briefly.

"There's a Miss Bailey, lives over by the Kellogs' across the bridge. She's an old maid who gives lessons. We'll go over and see her next Saturday and see how much she charges. If things go right, you can get started before your dad and me go into the camp at Bear Lake."

Miss Bailey proved to be quite a taskmaster. She was petite, prim, dressed in black, and altogether out of this world with a perpetual air of impatience about her that gave one the sense of having done something to upset her. Already full of fear and trepidation, I faced her for the first session—and almost wet myself. It all seemed so unreal, me standing awkwardly in front of this alien lady, apparently eager for my execution. I held by breath and waited.

"Take your violin out of its case, Lloyd," she said firmly. "Tighten your bow, apply your resin, and we shall begin."

She was a good lady, really, and any misgivings I had about her were slowly removed by my laboured advance along the road to tuneful playing. It was not easy, however, and being left-handed severely restricted my progress. But it was a right-handed world, and I just had to get used to it. Each week I crossed the bridge to Miss Bailey's house, and each week I got better and better. Then it happened. Chronically dissatisfied with my failure to tuck my left elbow under the instrument, she almost shouted "Tuck your arm in!" and gave a tug to emphasize her order. In went the elbow—and down went the violin, crashing to the floor. When I picked it up its face had cracked from its base to a point well beyond the bridge.

"Now see what you've done!" my teacher said.

I crept home with my broken symbol of respectability, secretly hoping that this would herald the end of my torture. But Mother saw it differently. "Alf," she said to Dad. "See what you can do to fix that fiddle. Then we'd better get packin' for camp. Lloyd, you're boardin' at Mrs. Evans, and she's expectin' you tomorrow. By the time we get back from camp, you'll be a fiddler for sure. Just remember, keep that elbow tucked in like Miss Bailey told you."

And so it was that by the following week I was back at Miss Bailey's sawing my way through "Twinkle, Twinkle Little Star" and other moving masterpieces of the music world. With growing confidence I began to see in Miss Bailey a kindly lady, a kindred spirit of my mother, whose only hope was that I would someday become a violinist—or, as my mother would say, a "real fiddler."

On impulse, I hitched a ride with an empty logging truck on its way back to the Bear Lake Camp.

"Wat'cha got in the box, Lloyd? Is that a machine-gun or somethin'?" asked "Snakey" Cooper, the driver.

"No," I answered. "It's my violin. I've been taking lessons from Miss Bailey over by the Kellogs'. Thought my mother and dad would like to hear me play."

"Well fancy that," mused Snakey. "Bessie Dennis has gone and got herself a real honest-to-goodness fiddler! I'll watch for you at the next square dance out at the hall."

Needless to say, Mother and Dad were pleased with my progress, and even my brother managed to say that I wasn't too bad for a "greenhorn." I was pleased to report this reaction to Snakey when I caught a ride back to town the next day.

"When you can play as good as your mother cooks, the whole town will turn out to hear ya!"

The Sunday school teacher had a brilliant idea. "We'll form an orchestra!" she chirped. "I'll play the piano, and Mac, Hans and Lloyd can play their violins. We'll just stick to easy pieces, ones that you all know—and aren't we fortunate that you can all read music?"

And that's why, on any given Sunday morning during the winter of 1938, the Lord could listen in and hear three impresarios sawing their way through "God Sees the Little Sparrow Fall," "Mothers of Salem" and "Jesus Loves Me," all accompanied by the sprightly teacher at the piano. History doesn't record what the Lord—or the world—thought of our efforts. But one thing is certain: we sure were proud of ourselves. And I know that my parents were, too.

Huntsville High School formed an orchestra at about the same time. I joined Gibby Antcliffe, Mac Avery, Helen Hutcheson and others to climb to loftier levels in the world of music. We were true pioneers. The school board had granted the school the huge sum of fifteen dollars to cover the costs involved, and we were on our self-conscious and halting way through the halls of harmony. And as time went by, we got better and better, till our principal would say to the world, "Yes we have our own orchestra—and it's quite good, too."

Helen played the cello. She was the daughter of one of the owners of the camps where my parents worked. Sometimes I walked her home after practice; and on such occasions, she was always nice to me, and although she wasn't my girlfriend, somehow it felt like I had taken one more step across the tracks.

I think that Mother thought so, too.

Beauty and the Bush

I couldn't believe my eyes. I looked at the note again. But no, there it was, in her small, neat script. "Dear Lloyd," it said. "My father won't allow me to see you anymore." Why, just the night before, we had lingered for the longest time in the hall of her stately home, discussing plans for the school dance. When I finally said good night, the biggest problem in the world was the fear that the war might end before I was old enough to win it for her and claim her as my wife. Now, without warning, my world had disappeared.

Ours had been a prudish kind of love affair. We skied a lot, but rarely took our skis off even to say good-night. One skiing outing remains cemented in my mind. On a beautiful winter night we were making our way across the ice to Scotch Bonnet Island, a beautiful tiny landmark on Fairy Lake, on the edge of town. Coming in the opposite direction were two shadowy young denizens from the west-end of town. There was no call of greeting; but as they receded into the night, one was heard to call out, "Why don't you take her out to the island and ..." And what he suggested that I do to her burned our sense of propriety to such a degree that the two of us remained silent for the remainder of the journey.

Oh, I was smitten, without doubt. Sometimes after a particular day of yearning I would get my skis out, and off I would go, weaving into the night. With my precious skis of Finnish purity, I would use them to purge my emotion, and by the time I'd reached home, both skis and suitor were too tired to pine any more. Bed and oblivion would take their turn.

My love for the girl was the sort that kindled all the fires of my overly active imagination. It was as if I found her the perfect foil for my idealistic and dramatic view of life, and I came to use it at the expense of other normal pursuits. As I grew older, two aims in life became predominant for me. One was to marry this girl. The other, to become a Spitfire pilot.

We skied together, walked together, went to parties together, and went infrequently to the show. When she delivered an oral composition on T.N.T. at school, I suffered as she stood in her neat plaid dress, her bosoms shaking in nervous reaction to the ordeal. When she stood fifth in the class to my fourteenth, I gladly bowed to her ability; and when she played the piano, I marvelled at her skill. When I took to painting, she was the object of my efforts. On page after page torn from the one-cent pad, I dashed off daily miniatures for her in water-colour, vowing to paint her a picture every day. This lofty pursuit took precedence over study, and my grades proved it. I had become possessed.

We often parted with agonizing argument, which sometimes took place in the back hall of her home. On such occasions, her father would periodically interrupt as he carried house plants to the coolness of the basement, and I could judge from his look that it was time to break off and go home. Had I more wisdom, I would have realized that the arguments had their roots in the torment that arose from constant struggle for acceptability. I was in over my head, as my mother described it, and my response was an irritability that was unhealthy for both of us.

We were poorly matched, in one respect. She was "upper crust," while I was among the scrapings of Huntsville's social pie. We had no home of our own. Worse, I was reduced to boarding in town while my parents worked in the war plant at Nobel. She practised figure skating at the local arena. I played hockey on the school's team. She played tennis and went to the library. I worked for Mr. Ginsberg in the Huntsville Trading Company. Her parents sat in the front pews at Church; my parents had sat at the back. They had a maid. I was a boarder.

It was a bad match, as they say. But I was sixteen and in love; and such social ingredients were of little significance, except to increase the ardour of my heart. I kept painting, and painting—until I got the note. Then I died inside.

I suffered the rest of the day, waiting for a chance to slip into the school's science room. Once there, I removed a small amount of carbon tetrachloride, then skied up into the bush behind the town's reservoir and zapped down a small amount of the poison. With great ceremony, I lay down beside my skis to die. By eleven o'clock, in fear of freezing to death, I went home to my bed.

"I can't even commit suicide," I moaned to myself. And more hurt was on its way. She wouldn't even speak to me, and would turn her head when we met in the hall, leaving me heartbroken. It was as if I had ceased to exist.

My plight was made more difficult because the rest of the world seemed not to notice, or even care. The bustling life of Huntsville

High went on as usual, with my friends chattering and giggling their way through the halls, completely oblivious to my devastation.

It got worse. We were both in the chorus of *Pinafore*, an operetta that the irrepressible Reverend Oaten had encouraged. We had already performed in Huntsville; and shortly after my rejection we were belting it out in Bracebridge. And when our leading lovelorn sailor plaintively wailed "Pale moon, to thee I sing, bright region of the Heavens ...," I was totally shattered. There was only one thing left to do.

And so it was that, shortly after we returned to Huntsville, and without saying goodbye to anyone, I hesitantly approached the principal. And that good and kindly man, already accustomed to leaves falling from the tree due to the winds of war, wished me luck. I was on my way into the "real world," as they say.

Get Yourself a Suit!

"Excuse me sir. May I please become a member?" The pretty girl stood at the counter expectantly, and waited hopefully with her companion. The young man rose from behind his desk and approached the counter.

"Certainly," he answered cheerfully. "Just fill out this form and sign it, and I'll prepare your card for you." In five minutes the deed was done; and as she left the office, he called after her. "Perhaps you might be interested in the show tonight. It starts at nine."

"Thank you," she answered cheerfully, "We just might do that—if you're paying." And off they went, giggling to themselves.

So there I was, so recently transformed from a high school dropout into a sixteen-year-old executive in the real word, complete with shirt, tie, jacket and shining shoes. The site of my transformation was the Malcolm Club, a recreational facility built expressly for the workers at the Defense Industries Plant in Nobel, just north of Parry Sound. I was one of two shift supervisors working eight-hour shifts between 8 a.m. and 12 midnight. A French-Canadian named Hervé Depatie was the other. Together, we supervised a complex which included a library, bowling alley, pool room, gymnasium, theatre, hockey pad, horseshoe pitch and tuck shop. It was a welcome mecca for the plant's thousands of employees, many of whom lived in the nearby camp. The two girls who had just signed up were part of the force that worked in the kitchens that served the camp.

For me, the transformation from lovelorn teenager to recreational supervisor was magical. Virtually overnight, I had abandoned my youthful life, full of friends and fantasies, and moved to another part of the country to become a full-fledged member of the adult world—with all the baggage that went with it. It was as if I had been launched to another planet—a comparison that wasn't even appropriate in those days! And it wasn't easy. To begin with, my parents had to deal with what, to them, was a family calamity of major proportions. They were housed in a tent-trailer on a farm on the edge of Parry Sound until Dad finished the tiny houses that he was building for themselves and my brother's family, and had little room to spare. More importantly, they were faced with the question of what to do with me. To say that they were shocked would be the understatement of the day.

"You'll go to school in Parry Sound," said Mother.

"No," said I, "I've finished with school. I'm here to work until I'm old enough to join the army." And that settled the matter.

Dad knew a man in the office who knew Mr. Buchanan, the director of the Malcolm Club. He'd start the wheels turning. When I appeared as a candidate before the director of the Malcolm Club, I could hardly believe it. "You're hired," he said. "Now, your partner Mr. Depatie will explain your duties—and good luck!—and get yourself a suit!"

The shock continued. A Commissioner was posted at the door on guard, and custom decreed that he be a Great War veteran. So there I was, on my first day of duty, confronted by this ramrod figure of military correctness, complete with uniform, medals and handle-bar mustache, standing at attention and almost shouting, "Welcome aboard, sir! I'm at your service!"

The reader can well imagine my reaction. Why, it seemed like only moments ago I was a brash young teenager asking my Uncle Henry stupid questions about a long-ago war; now here I was, being saluted by one of his old comrades! His name was Mr. Foley, and as time went on, I found that his very presence did wonders for the Club's decorum—and my growing sense of maturity. So did the high-spirited Mary Greenwood, who served as secretary. She was another of my instructors on the new road to adulthood, and I remember her as a wise and friendly teacher in the subject of human relationships.

Shortly after I had been transformed, I found that my recent sense of defeat was about to be revived. Huntsville's popular production of *H.M.S. Pinafore* was booked to appear at the Malcolm Club. The fateful night arrived; and there, midst stage props and costumed players, was my lost love, singing merrily along as one of the sisters, cousins or aunts of Pinafore's Captain. I stepped out while the hero bayed at the moon; but I doubt if she even knew that I was there. And my pain was dulled by Commissioner Foley. At least he showed me some respect!

It was customary at the end of the day to collect the cash box from the bowling alley and deposit it in the office filing cabinet for safe-keeping. On the day in question, I paid little attention to the quiet individual that shadowed me about as the day wound down. He offered to help with any tasks that needed attention, and stood casually by as I put away the cash box and prepared to go home. I gave him little note.

The next morning I got a frantic visit from Hervé Depatie. "You must come quickly, Lloyd," he almost shouted. "The cash box has been stolen. I have already told Monsieur Foley. But you must come."

And so it was that two upset supervisors rushed to the scene of the crime. By some sudden logic, we decided to begin the search for the cash box across the road, in the camp. And by some strange quirk of fate we found it, deposited in a garbage container just inside the first building. Talk about luck! Although it was empty, we rushed triumphantly back to our office eager to report the theft to the police.

We found them already there. Without explanation, they escorted us up to the main gatehouse and placed us in a line-up. Still wondering what it was all about, we faced a small, older man who passed along the line. Stopping before Hervé and me, he pointed his finger and said, "That's them!" It turned out that the man who identified us was the caretaker of the building where we discovered the box. He put two and two together, got six, and reported us as the thieves. In due course, it was all sorted out. The suspected thief—my shadow of the night before—was identified, caught and charged just as he was leaving town, and Hervé and I were vindicated.

Strangely, the Malcolm Club director, Mr. Buchanan, was replaced shortly thereafter by a French-Canadian. Hervé remained, but I was transferred to the gatehouse, and made responsible for the escort of various delivery trucks to cafeterias and refreshment booths within the well-guarded munitions plant. I was sorry to leave my job at the club, and missed my daily camaraderie with Mr. Foley and the jovial manager of the bowling alley. His name was Tom Hoddy, and he had a wooden leg. But that didn't stop him from telling me tall tales of his days in the navy.

Oh, and the girl who bought the membership? Her name was Dorothy Schwartz. We were married just before I joined the army.

Strangers in our Midst

It was May 10, 1942, and I was the proud owner of a new car. It wasn't really new, of course. It was a 1932 Pontiac coupé, complete with rumble seat, overdrive shift, and hubcaps that sparkled in the sun. To me, it was the chariot of my dreams. I had purchased it from a young doctor who had just joined the army; and it stood there, almost begging to be taken on a trial run.

Why not? I thought. It's Sunday, my day off at the Defence Plant. A "good run" will do us both good. Since I was a recent émigré from Muskoka, perhaps a return trip, even for a moment, would be good for the soul. Gravenhurst seemed like a good idea. Mother, who also worked at Nobel and missed her Muskoka roots, offered to pack a lunch and join me on the journey.

"We could go by the Sanatorium and visit Tina for a little while. It would be good for her."

Muskoka had become renowned for its pure, bracing air; and long before I saw the light of day, its reputation had resulted in the construction of sanatoria for "consumptives," as those afflicted with tuberculosis were called. They stretched along the heights of Muskoka Bay on the northern outskirts of Gravenhurst, and were filled to capacity with patients from the United States and Canada. Tina Sproat was in one of these. Her roots went back to the early settlement of Muskoka, and my mother was a long-time friend. She beamed at the thought of seeing Tina Sproat again.

The trip seemed to grow more exciting as we entered my "homeland." Parry Sound, well, it was equally beautiful, but it just wasn't the same, somehow. I even felt that the car ran better as we entered Bala and headed south toward Gravenhurst; and at the time we reached its outskirts, I was sure of it. Then something happened that put a whole new spin on the trip.

As we proceeded up the street from the bay, we were stopped in our tracks by a commotion up ahead. Getting out of the car, I approached the bystanders at the curb and stared at the cause of their curiosity. There, within twenty feet, was a group of German prisoners being marched from the train to the camp that waited for them on the edge of town. And contrary to what one might expect under such circumstances, they were striding along defiantly, singing a wartime song known only to them. Dressed in remnants of air force, army and naval uniforms, they were an untidy lot; but considering their recent misadventures, one could hardly expect more.

It was only 1942, of course, and these prisoners still had every hope of winning the war. As far as they were concerned, a brief rest "on the shores of beautiful Lake Muskoka" before returning to win the war would be almost as beneficial as a stay in the neighbouring sanatorium.

The Canadian guards accompanying the prisoners looked resolute and every bit in charge, and I felt a surge of pride as I realized that according to my plan, I would be joining the Army at the end of summer. Then I might have an opportunity to see more Germans—from a different perspective. I waited till they and their songs departed, then returned to my mother and the car. As we continued north along the cliffs to the Muskoka Hospital and Tina Sproat, I felt different somehow. And even the busy chatter of those two old friends failed to alter my mood. I couldn't get my mind off those prisoners.

For the past two years, I had been so busy with my own problems. These included rejected love, dropping out of school, and moving away to begin work. I had no time to pay attention to things that were happening beyond the end of my nose. In the midst of these personal adventures, beautiful Muskoka had opened its gates to prisoners of war—and I had scarcely noticed! By the time my mother and I encountered a group of them on their way from the train to the camp, it had already been operating there for two years.

These prisoners were fortunate. Of all the Allied prison camps, Number 20 at Gravenhurst was the best. Unofficially called "Calydor" after is former use as a private sanatorium, it occupied a beautiful height of land overlooking Muskoka Bay. Passing steamers and other craft were in full view, and the prisoners were allowed to swim in a marked-off area of the lake. They even had access to Eaton's catalogue, and several of them took advantage of it by using their meagre allowance to order necessities. One enterprising prisoner purchased an Underwood typewriter from Eaton's—paid for in installments, of course!

By all accounts, the men took full advantage of their inviting surroundings, building an aquarium and a tennis court, which served as a skating rink in winter. A more remarkable adventure was the development of a farm about three miles north of the camp. This creative endeavour resulted from a fire that destroyed the farmhouse. The inventive commandant of the camp arranged to lease the property—and the rest was history. The prisoners maintained stock and grew produce, which found its way to the tables of the camp. But more importantly, the farm helped keep active a number of healthy men, who might otherwise have been driven to less productive schemes.

Calydor is gone now. All that remains are bits of crumbling concrete hidden in the growth of time. The site is designated as a building project, and even those mute marks of Muskoka's history will be gone, along with the men who lived there over fifty years ago.

By odd coincidence, a book which I have tells the story of Calydor from a prisoner's point of view. He was Hans-Georg Neumann, who returned after the war to live in Canada. In *A Man Worth Knowing*, he wrote that he arrived in Gravenhurst on the day of the Pentecost in May 1942. Could he have been among those whom I saw on that May day? I'll never know.

Mr. Cecil Porter, of Gravenhurst, has written an interesting book about Camp Calydor from the Canadian viewpoint, titled *The Gilded Cage: Gravenhurst German Prisoner-of-War Camp 20, 1940-1946.*

Sam Browne's Belt

It was the fall of 1942, and I could still hear the call of that billboard, "You too, can join the Air Force!" And it became clearer with the arrival of a boarder at our tiny house in Parry Sound. He, too, worked at the Defence Plant, and Mother took him in out of pity. His name was Roy Corner. His home was in Toronto, and he was quick to tell me that World War I hero Billy Bishop was his uncle.

"You're always talking about becoming a pilot," he said. "Why not go to the recruiting office in Toronto, and join the Air Force? You could stay overnight at my house, pass on our regards to Uncle Billy, and be on your way."

My pulse quickened. With the reluctant blessings of my parents, I rushed to Toronto and glory. But my chance at being a pilot was shot down by an eye test right off the bat, and I crept home with my tail between my legs. The army would have to do.

B136980 Private Dennis, L.A., having endured the orientation of recruitment at Toronto's Canadian National Exhibition grounds, moved on to the basic training camp at Brantford. Here I was placed in an x-group designated for six weeks of training instead of eight. Naturally, it was a right-handed army, and I had a little trouble with the rifle drill. But I became a marksman, and could play regular soldier with the best of them. By good luck, I even had dinner one weekend with Reverend Beverley Oaten, who was now pastor of the Park Street United Church in Brantford. But this is the story of Sam Browne's belt, not a litany of my adventures in basic training; so I must move on.

When the six weeks were up, I moved on to Camp Borden—and this is where it happened. At the end of my advanced training, I expected to go on embarkation leave and head overseas. I went home on leave alright, but it was just a weekend pass; when I got back to Borden, I found that I'd been made a corporal. The draft left without me.

A short time later I was called off parade with several others, including a sergeant and sergeant-major. We formed a group outside the administration building and were tersely told that we had been selected for officer training and would be leaving immediately for Three Rivers, Quebec!

The officers' course at Three Rivers was really two courses. The first was a preliminary process of weeding out the undesirables by the most tortuous tests of endurance the army could devise. Successful candidates then graduated to the course proper, and became Officer Cadets, willing, if not ready, to begin the process of elimination all over again.

Bit by gruelling bit that summer, I took on the markings of a young officer; and although those markings would require time and experience to burnish them, a close observer could see them as new growth, something that was not there a year before. A letter home provides evidence of that personal development.

Three Rivers
July 30, 1943

Dear Folks:

It certainly seems a long time since I joined the army, which was really only eight months ago! So much has happened and I'm not even overseas yet!

You asked about the course I'm taking. Well, it's pretty difficult, I must say. We have a lot of theory about tactics, troop movements, gun placements, that sort of thing. One question asked us to calculate the angle of elevation for a gun to shoot a shell over a hill of a certain height. (I sure could have used a little more math from High School!) But the hardest part is the physical. From running to rope climbing and obstacle courses, we are kept constantly on the move. Today, for instance, we had to run a distance while wearing our gas masks, then pull them off and make an impromptu speech! I was given the topic "The Woman's Place is in the Home," some war subject, eh? Ask Mom what she thinks of that!

Three Rivers is an interesting place and I am glad that Dorothy was able to come to stay here while I am on course. We are able to go bike riding and sightseeing whenever I am free—which isn't often! Last weekend we went up to Quebec City by boat. There was a big commotion around the Château Frontenac Hotel, and people said that Churchill and Roosevelt were meeting there. They didn't invite us in, though!

Get that barracks box ready Dad! I'll need it to carry all these beautiful socks Mom keeps sending me! With luck, I should graduate here at the end of August. Then I'll be home for a short leave, and order you all around!

Your loving son,
Lloyd.

On a bright and shining day early in September I stood with my companions before the reviewing stand in the Exhibition Park at Three Rivers and accepted my commission from our Defence Minister, Colonel J.L. Ralston:

GEORGE THE SIXTH, by the Grace of God, of Great Britain, Ireland and the British Dominions beyond the Seas, King, Defender of the Faith, Emperor of India.

To Our Trusty and well beloved Cadet Lloyd Arthur Dennis Greetings. We, reposing especial Trust and Confidence in your Loyalty, Courage and good Conduct do by these presents Constitute and Appoint you to be an Officer in our Army of our Dominion of Canada from the Eleventh day of September, 1943. You are therefore carefully and diligently to discharge your duty as such in the Rank of 2nd Lieutenant or in such other Rank as We may from time to time hereafter be pleased to promote or appoint you to of which a notification will be made in the Canadian Gazette, or in such other manner as may for the time being be prescribed by Us in Council, and you are in such manner and on such occasions as may be prescribed by Us to exercise and well discipline in Arms, both the Inferior Officers, and Men serving under you and use your best endeavours to keep them in good Order and Discipline. And We do hereby Command them to Obey you as their superior Officer, and you to observe and follow such Orders and Directions as from time to time you shall receive from Us, or any of your superior Officers, according to the Rules and Discipline of War, in pursuance of the Trust hereby reposed on you.

Second Lieutenant Dennis put on his new officer's uniform complete with shining buttons, brown shoes, Sam Browne belt and officer's cap. He picked up his new officer's swagger stick with his right hand, and headed for home.

It was dark and windy as I crossed the parade square after dinner in the officers' mess. Now back in Camp Borden to qualify for the second "pip" of a first lieutenant, I was barely beyond the aura of graduation, and unused to this new role. A figure passed me, almost invisible in the darkness. Suddenly I heard a call, still strange when addressed to me.

"Sir!"

I turned to find a sergeant-major striding toward me.

"What is it, sergeant-major?"

"What it is, sir," he said sarcastically, "is that you failed to return my salute when I passed you. As superior officer, you are required by King's Regulations to return the salute of all subordinate ranks."

I explained that I was new at this business, and had forgotten.

"Well sir," he said, "you're an officer now, and you better get used to it. Next time I salute, you'd bloody well better salute back." He again saluted, and after waiting for me to return the compliment, turned about and strode off into the darkness.

My fine new armour cracked and, just for a moment, I felt like a kid again.

The barracks box mentioned in my letter was something that my dad promised me, should I become an officer. And Sam Browne's Belt? It was introduced into the British army by Colonel Sam

Browne at the end of the nineteenth century. Originally intended to support the weight of an officer's sword, it had long become a symbol, part of an officer's dress uniform trappings. I still have mine.

Stand Up! Hook Up! Check Your Equipment!

It was in August 1944 that I saw two notices on the bulletin board of the Officers' Mess in Peterborough. One was in response to the loss of officers suffered by the British Army thus far. It announced a Can-Loan Program, inviting young Canadian officers to go on loan to the British Army. The other was an invitation to volunteer for the First Canadian Parachute Battalion. "Successful candidates could be overseas within weeks of graduation!" said the notice.

Since receiving my commission, I had been chafing at the bit. Serving time as an instructor was fair enough—for a while. But I'd been doing it for a year. If I didn't get over soon—well the whole thing would be over! Now, unexpectedly, there seemed to be a way out. Joining another man's army seemed far less exciting than jumping down upon the enemy in a Canadian uniform—and it held a further attraction: if I couldn't fly an aircraft, at least I could jump from one. I applied that very day.

It wasn't as easy as it sounded. First I had to go to the Osborne Barracks at Winnipeg and pass a gruelling number of mental and physical tests, designed to weed out all but the most likely candidates; and I immediately was struck by their severity. They made the officer-cadet tests look like child's play! I desperately hoped that the results would prove me worthy, and when the officer nodded and said, "You're in!" I almost kissed him. Now, it was off to Camp Shilo, not far from Brandon, Manitoba. I caught the train and headed west.

While in Winnipeg, I had gleaned some information about the First Canadian Parachute Battalion. I learned that it had been formed in 1942 from hand-picked officers and N.C.O.s. They had first trained in Fort Benning, Georgia, and later moved to the new facility at Shilo, Manitoba. They were an elite, highly trained force, which had already gained the admiration of both the allies and the enemy during their jump on D-Day in June 1944. Their reputation had grown to legendary proportions, and had spread to permeate their reinforcement base to which I was now attached. Added to this reputation as a fighting force was its distinctive dress. The maroon beret and gleaming jump boots were symbols of distinction that each member wore proudly. And, like those of the airmen, the jumpers' wings identified them with the new air age of war.

When I walked into the Officers' Mess on that first day, the behaviour of my hosts was so bizarre that I was not quite certain what to do. One lieutenant was standing on his hands in the corner, while another lay on the floor with his feet stretched up along the wall. A small deer stood in the middle of the carpet, while through the hall strode an officer on skis, complete with mitts and parka. It turned out to be a brief display of madness, designed to quicken the pulse of a psychiatrist who was expected momentarily. He was from the testing unit at Winnipeg where I had been processed, and was making a routine visit. They were about to "pull his leg" as they say. They certainly succeeded in pulling mine!

I had entered the rare world of extreme endurance. A newcomer on the field of battle whose whole purpose was to fight *behind* enemy lines, it seemed obvious that the paratroopers' preparation for such a daring task should be arduous in the extreme. A certain élan pervaded the place, and every task, from calisthenics to running, had an added edge to it. It certainly was no place for weaklings, as I was soon to discover.

When finally it became my turn to have my mettle tested, I donned a pair of coveralls and became indistinguishable from the other ranks in the squad. But the instructors knew who among us were officers, and took unusual delight in extracting just a little more agony from our bodies than from the other ranks. That seemed fair. An officer should expect to endure as much as his men—and a little bit more. I took it in stride; and when my forty push-ups never seemed to satisfy Sergeant "Moose" McGannon, I gave him ten more without complaint.

After endless practice at long-distance running, rope climbing, unarmed combat, calisthenics, cable jumping, jumping from moving trucks, learning how to fall and roll, we were finally ready to jump from the tower. Here again I fell victim to the sergeant's humour. One exercise consisted of drawing the trainee up the tower cable in a head down position. On command, the student released himself and fell freely for a distance while changing a ball from one hand to the other. I was drawn up and left hanging there while the sergeant broke the men off for a smoke!

Finally, after three weeks of such conditioning, we were led to the Packing Hangar. Here we watched as female members of the army carefully folded parachutes on long tables.

"Be nice to these girls, men," said the sergeant. "Nowhere in the world are women more deserving of your respect and kind attention, for they hold your lives in their hands. Who knows? The one you are looking at may even now be packing your chute for tomorrow's jump! Look upon her with beseeching eyes, and hope to God you live to see her again! Alright! Let's go!"

"Stand up!" The jump instructor shouted to make himself heard over the roar of the plane's engines.

"Hook up!" We snapped our straps to the cable running the length of the plane.

"Check your equipment!" I checked my harness, and the chute on the back of the man in front.

"Sound off for equipment check"

"One okay!" "Two okay!" Successively, we called out the results of our safety check.

"Close up, and stand in the door!"

Until that morning, I had never even been near an airplane. Then, in a rush of mounting excitement, we had been ordered aboard this Lockheed Lodestar, which to me seemed the biggest plane in the world. A hair-raising orientation flight had followed, which left many of us eager to leave the aircraft by any means possible. Swooping and climbing, the pilot managed to make several men part with their breakfasts before he finally levelled off twelve hundred feet above the drop zone. What we had trained so hard for was about to be tested.

"Ready! Ho!" The jump master tapped me lightly on the leg and I was out and away.

We had been taught to say "one t'ousand, two t'ousand, tree t'ousand" in the interval before the chute opened, carefully dropping the "h" lest we bite our tongue with the sudden jolt of the chute. I'm afraid that I blasphemed, and only managed an agonizing "Jesus Christ!" before Bang! The silk snapped open over my head, and I felt the euphoria awarded all jumpers as I blissfully drifted down, halfway between heaven and earth.

Bump! I hit the prairie, collapsed my chute and stood up. With a rare sense of elation I gathered my chute and headed for the waiting truck. My self-confidence had just been given another boost.

After graduation, I was frustrated to learn that instead of being posted in overseas draft, I was assigned as an instructor in the trained soldier company. Arranging for Dorothy to move to the nearby city of Brandon, I settled in to the gruelling routine of the endless training of troops. Since training including running, we platoon leaders regularly ran our men to and from Brandon, and vied with one another for the best time. I was especially proud when my men did it in just over three hours. The distance was about twenty miles.

The field exercises were made especially rigorous by the severity of winter and the expectations demanded of airborne troops. Casualty rates seemed unreasonably high, notwithstanding. Although only one or two were killed while jumping during my period there, considerably more were killed by a variety of other accidents. Visiting the hospital as Orderly Officer one day, I was dismayed to find a younger trooper lying with his head in a brace. He had broken his neck swinging from the steam pipes in the hut, and died a few days later. More to be expected, we had our quota of broken bones, sprains and concussions. I had kept a knee injury to myself since the last jump, lest it spoil my chances for a draft.

By this time I had become good friends with my fellow officers, and when Captain Furlotte was put on draft, I very much wished that I could go with him. It was not to be. He made it in time to take part in the Varsity drop over the Rhine in March 1945. On VE day I was still stuck in Shilo.

So much for that notice on the billboard!

Home is Where the Heart Is

Alfred and Bessie Dennis were typical of many young Canadian couples who started out in the early years of the twentieth century. They were ready for adventure and prepared to move wherever fortune beckoned. Married in 1914 in the Muskoka Lakes district, they were drawn almost immediately by expanding growth of Sudbury. My older brother was born there in 1918.

But for them, fortune seemed built upon shifting sands, and by the time I arrived, they were working at a mill in the bush of Muskoka—Mother as a cook and Dad as a time-keeper and scaler of logs. We lived in a ramshackle old building that also served as a cook-house and dining area for the men; and one could safely say that, from the moment of birth, I was surrounded by the rough and tumble adventure of life in the bush. There were few amenities, either for my mother or for me; and my idea of a crowd was provided by a flock of hens that was part of the cook's inventory. A mountain of sawdust became my playground, and Mother and Dad found solace in the nearby village of Aspdin where they formed a bond with friends that remained strong throughout their lives.

Four years later, we were in a tiny rented house in Martin's Siding, four miles away. It had a mill, too, right across the road. But a home is more than a house, and I soon found out that Martin's Siding offered much more than the mill at Aspdin. It boasted a tiny general store that sold everything from coal oil to cookies. It was also the post office, and its pot-bellied stove was a magnet for men, particularly in winter. Just past the store was the railway track. It was there that I first saw the trains that would wend their way throughout much of my life. There was a station, and a siding to serve the nearby mill for the log cars. When a hobo knocked on our door one day, Mother gave him a meal—and I got a quick lesson in humanity. Less than a mile away was a school ready and waiting for "lefty Lloyd," as I was called; and even closer lay Mud Lake, an enticing trap for small boys, while surrounding fields, loaded with berries, held an open invitation to Mother. And just as Mother and her sons were becoming addicted to berries and bathing, circumstances called us away to another world, in a place called Ullswater.

The house stood in a clearing by the road, less than a mile from Skeleton Lake. Dad had built it himself, and it had the pride of my parents written all over it. The land and the lumber were part of the employment deal made with the owner, Mr. Bert Simms. A handshake was given in lieu of a deed.

Ullswater had everything that boys could want—a swimming hole, a blacksmith shop, a nice school, forests, fields and friends. Mother became renowned for her baking, and Dad for his skill at bookkeeping and scaling lumber. But our luck ran out when the Depression crept in. Bert Simms went down—and took Dad with him. The family was scattered like leaves as we shot the dog and moved away.

Utterson was my next home. Really, it was an upstairs room in the Bain house where Mother cared for the elderly owners. Dad and my brother headed north to look for work. Utterson could be best described as an eye-opener for me. The village had several stores, a blacksmith shop, a gas station, a hotel, an ice cream parlour, a church—and even a hall and fairground. Many of the townsfolk had inside toilets—and the school had two rooms. I had really come up in the world.

But six months later fortune carried us off to a lodge in Peninsula Lake, where Mother was hired as cook. And just as I was getting used to living in a tiny room over the kitchen and the new kids at the Canal school, I was whisked away again to board at the farm of the Earls in Aspdin, back in the land of my birth. It only lasted for a month in the fall, but I got to share a bed with Sid and Bill, and the latter and I became bonded in our regular job of "going for the cows." Mr. Hammell was the teacher, and one day when he called my name, there was no answer. I had been called away to Falkenburg, where Mother went to cook for Moore's Mill. Once again I was confined to a tiny room in a strange place, and faced the trial of making new friends. My "catapult," or sling-shot, became my bonding agent, and soon I was knocking off insulators with the best of them!

But by December I had to say good-bye to teacher Miss Helvi Macki and my new friends in Falkenburg and move to the grandest place of all—the town of Huntsville! I was put to board with Pat and Hazel Brooks, on the edge of the town. They were kindly landlords —but my introduction to urbanity did not go well. In my winter breeks and rubbers, I felt out of place among these town mice, and I lasted only a week before running away to the logging camp where my family had gone to work.

Ravensworth was Heaven. An isolated speck on the side of the tracks, it was the site of a Muskoka Wood Company camp—and a temporary home of the whole Dennis family. But it had all the tonic ingredients to quench the thirst of a boy who needed a sense of belonging. The teacher was kindly, and the children a small mixture of French and Finnish-Canadians who became my friends. A Finnish father made me a pair of skis, complete with rawhide harness. I went for a sauna every Saturday night, and vicariously fed upon the adventurous life of a logging camp. I was kindly monitored by Tom, the philosopher-flunkey of the cook, and met the train when it stopped each week. Best of all was the sense of belonging that I got from being with my family. My bed was a tiny upper bunk over that of my parents at the back of the cook-house, but my home was the whole camp; and I loved it.

Then, one fine spring day, the train stopped and plucked us up like fruit for the market. It trundled over the trestle and up to the junction, where we caught another that rushed us back to Huntsville. Back to the world of town mice we moved, into a rented house on the edge of town; and I found some comfort in the fact that at least it had the luxury of an outdoor toilet and coal-oil lamps. But I refused to go back to the town school. Instead, I opted for the long walk to the country school at the Locks, and it was a wise choice. As far as the house went, it failed miserably in its attempt to leave a lasting impression on me. It still sits there, more than sixty years later, seemingly impervious to improvement or dilapidation. It's just a house.

The same cannot be said of my next home in Huntsville. A mean, stark box of bricks, it stood in a row with its sisters, on the bank of the street in the west end of the town. Together, they were called the Parliament houses, not after a namesake in Ottawa, but after the man who owned them. The only good thing I could say about that house was its view over Hunter's Bay. It was magnificent! The sisters are all gone now, and I can only say good riddance!

When my parents moved to Nobel for work in the war plant in 1940, I was put to board with Mrs. Evans. And I must say that she made that tiny cabin on the Brunel Road really seem like home. She fussed over me far beyond my needs; and that pleased my mother, who had left me only because she wanted me to finish school and "make something of myself."

But a little note from my girlfriend shattered me one day. I said goodbye to youth and joined my parents in the world of work. Crowded into an old trailer and spilling into a tent attached, we survived the first fall of snow before Dad finished two tiny houses—one for us and one for my brother Vernon and his wife, Marg. Built on borrowed land, they sat like tiny twins on the road leading up to the friendly farmer who would own them when we left. But for the moment, they were home to the family; and even with the backhouse shared outside, my house was a cozy and heart-warming place, and I was proud to call it home when I left to join the army.

All Aboard!

Long before I saw one, I heard its wailing call in the night, sweeping across the bush as it rushed on its way across our great country. *Whooo-ooo!* it would howl, and as the sound gradually waned to a moan and finally disappeared, it always left me wondering what this great machine was really like. Dad had described the train to me, and I had seen pictures in Eaton's catalogue. I had even prayed that Santa Claus would bring me one. But he never did. And it was not till we moved to Martin's Siding that I finally saw one, puffing and wheezing, as it stood for a moment at the tiny station. What a truly monstrous beast it was, with its long barrel of a belly resting on giant wheels, all standing in a row while clinging to the rails!

A curious bulge hung by its front sides, and long arms reached to hang on the rims of the giant wheels. At its front the beast was fitted with a curious iron nose just above the tracks. Called a cow-catcher, it was a ghoulish guard against cows that might wander into its path. And higher up was a light that beamed into the night. And there, on top, was the whistle, the cause of that noise that I had heard in the night.

Suddenly, from the door of one of the line of matching cars, a voice called, "All Aboard!" The whistle gave a tremendous blast, and the bulge below the belly of the train hissed loudly. The great arms pushed against the wheels until they slowly began to move. The train was on its way. Slowly at first, then with increasing speed, the cars swept by like segments of a snake, clackety-clack, clackety-clack, they clattered in a curious harmony made by the joints in the rails. And long after the train had disappeared, it could be heard winding its way into the distance. It was a powerful, compelling experience, that first clear view of a train. And it would come back repeatedly in one way or another to become a regular visitor in my life. Sometimes its visit was happy, sometimes sad. But it was there; and it planted itself so firmly in my mind that the train has become a powerful presence in my memory.

It was inevitable that the train would weave its way into the Canadian fabric. Forty years before I first saw one, trains had found their way clear across the country, and tracks had begun to reach out like veins across the body of the land. Many depended upon the railway for their livelihood, and thousands of young children like me became weaned on the milk supplied by the rails. After the British custom, it was known as the railway. And it rubbed shoulders so intimately with the American "railroads" that it still has a hard time keeping the proper name. Even as I write this, today's local paper calls out to note a Canadian tale of "railroad" history; and the little boy in me peeps, "It's rail*way*, stupid!"

The railway became a favourite companion of my brother and our friends at Martin's Siding during our brief stay there. We'd place our ears on the rails and listen for incoming trains, still miles away. We'd walk the rails to school, foolishly claiming to be the last to leave in the face of an approaching train. A penny would be placed on the rails, to have its face obliterated by the passing giant, and we were not above begging a piece of pie from the cook of the work train on the odd occasions when it was parked on the siding. And hobos, or "tramps," became more frequent on the passing freights, as times got hard. I remember setting out a little table and chair for one when he came up the road to our house. Mother fed him royally. "It's him today—might be my man tomorrow," was her sentiment.

Mother, of course, had an earlier and less exciting experience with trains. As a young girl in Allensville she and her siblings had to load bark and slabwood onto railway cars before going to school. And years later, when a train carried her into the logging camp in Ravensworth, its lone passenger car could hardly be called a chariot headed for happiness.

I got to see the business end of that same car in my turn. When I ran away from school in Huntsville in 1936, it was Canada's railway network that made it possible. I hopped on the Northland when it stopped in town, got off fifteen miles north at Scotia Junction, boarded that same car when it came through on the Booth Railway, and was with my mother and dad by one o'clock in the morning. By such vicarious experience I became more familiar with the railway world and its relationship with lumber and logs. In such a setting, the train took on a living quality, almost like the teams of horses that were the first in the family of lumbermen and loggers.

For a moment during my early high school years, I came even closer to the business end of the train. It was my job to go to the station and load freight onto the baggage car when it stopped at the platform at three in the morning. It was a job, and I thought little of it. The lumbering train and the slip of a teenager had become friends through circumstances; and meeting it was a lot more pleasant than meeting Postmaster Mayhew later that morning. At least the train never ordered me around!

It was a train that carried me proudly to Hamilton and Older Boys' Parliament in 1939; and it took me to Toronto in 1942 when I tried to join the Air Force. Patiently it stood as I kissed my wife and family goodbye when I left to join the army, and regularly carried me home whenever I had leave. It slipped up on one such occasion. I was going home for Christmas, and slept through my stop at Parry Sound. Imagine my dismay when I awoke to see Nobel slipping by! The kindly conductor made certain that I got off at Britt, about thirty miles to the north. It was hours before I caught one of its sisters going south. I always stayed awake after that!

And so, the trains of Canada lugged me—and thousands of other servicemen—back and forth in sickness and in snow, from the one end of the country to the other. And ages later, when we had children of our own, I saw to it that they would get to meet the train. We put Gale and Susan on board the train at Huntsville, with orders to watch for us at every crossing. As they waved goodbye, we drove off and waited at each crossing as they swept by proudly. They joined us at Bracebridge and begged us to do it again. They were eight and ten years old. Six years later, they went to Vancouver and back and even stopped to visit the Calgary Stampede! That's what they call riding the rails.

The glory days of the trains are over now. And I can't help feeling that one day we may regret saying good bye to so many of our faithful iron horses.

The Play's the Thing!

More than fifty years after I had been rejected by my high school girlfriend, I lay in the Barrie Hospital, weak and weary following a bout with cancer and blood clots. Despite the care bestowed by my loved ones, I felt defeated and depressed. Then a phone call delivered an elixir that few patients get to savour.

"Hello, my name is Stina Nyquist. I'm calling from Huntsville. I've just read your memoir, *Marching Orders*, which includes some of your adventures while growing up around Huntsville. I am a playwright, and I wonder if you would allow me to write a play based upon your book. We could present it at the Muskoka Festival next year."

Would I mind! I can only say that Stina's call had all the power of a sip from the fountain of youth! I felt as though I had suddenly left the bed, to float sublimely out of the hospital and into a state of exaltation. One might wonder at this reaction, and sense an exaggeration in the telling; but the thought of my family and their heroic struggle reappearing in public to reveal themselves in vindication of their lowly circumstances was pretty heady stuff, especially in my physical and emotional state at the time.

Stina Nyquist was no trifler, either. She had already earned her reputation as the playwright of the area, and her works had provided quality entertainment at the Festival for some years. Always geared to local interest, her plays had a reputation of craftsmanship and talent. To attract her interest was an honour in itself, and I felt it keenly. I told her so.

Although *Marching Orders* is a memoir reaching through the years to my first days as a teacher, it is largely a literary journey through the adventurous years of my growing up in Muskoka. Huntsville was the vortex of that adventure, and many of my family's fortunes depended upon the work generated there and in the surrounding bush. Since those fortunes imposed constantly changing circumstances upon the life of a boy reaching toward adulthood and a world calamity, it was great fodder for a playwright with the insight to see both the wit and pathos that it contained. Stina Nyquist knew what she was about; she produced a script that plucked the essential strings to strum a simple ballad of youthful redemption. It had all the ingredients of the *Grapes of Wrath* and *Oliver Twist* mixed together. And when she selected the cast, it was as if she had known my family. As my mother would say, "She had us down to a 'T'."

Unless one has experienced it, the feeling of seeing a public portrayal of your family's trials, tribulations and triumphs is hard to grasp. When the curtain was drawn on opening night, there before my eyes were my mother, my dad, my grandmother, my brother, and even my dog, Jumbo. Deep feelings of emotion welled within me, and overflowed onto my cheeks. The cast was good; but Cheryl Taylor, the actor who portrayed my mother, cast such a spell that she swept me instantly into the past, where I remained throughout the performance. Even the fall of the final curtain failed to break the spell of that first night; and I went home with the strange feeling that my family would be waiting for tea when I got there.

The other ingredient that added a special flavour to the experience was the site chosen for the play. It was in the theatre of the town hall, where I had once briefly performed as a teenager during a high school initiation night. On a lower floor, I had once worked before school in the town's post office. But the crowning experience was to see in the audience many of my former friends and classmates, at least three of whom were portrayed in the story. They shared my enthusiastic response to the drama which unfolded. This included not only the trauma of my rejection by my beloved, but also my eventual emergence as a young paratroop officer, the pride and joy of his loving parents.

But my love of long ago was absent. Indeed, I hadn't seen her since the day I had quit school more than fifty years earlier. My erstwhile best friend, Vern Payne, was there, however. In fact, he was there for every performance through two seasons of the play's life. To my earlier comment that this person had not appeared and in fact was not expected, he replied, "Oh, she'll be here one night, that's for sure. You may not see her, but she'll be here. I'll bet your last dollar on it."

My good friend Vern was right, as always. Toward the end of the play's run, while I was signing books in the lobby, she opened, perhaps in hope of an unobtrusive exit, a rear door against my signing table. She seemed as surprised as I. There we were, two senior citizens, bereft of skis and interest in each other. After awkward pleasantries, she chided me for the play's portrayal of her.

"You show me being helped by you with my geography homework. I would like you to know that I majored in geography at university." She failed to mention any other aspect of our earlier life, or the trauma that I suffered by her rejection. Beyond telling me that she and her sons had cottages on a nearby lake where they were residing for the summer, she had little to say. I can't remember whether she bought a book. But she knows the story. After all, she saw the play.

Letter to a Muskoka Teacher

Dear Miss Fenn:

I don't know whether you ever read the Education Act concerning the duties of teachers, or even the excerpt that was repeated in the front of the classroom register. It read, in part: "... to inculcate, by precept and example—the highest regard for truth, justice, loyalty, love of country, humanity, benevolence, sobriety, industry, frugality, purity, temperance and all other virtues."

One can well imagine the author's torment upon composing that section. Surely, such a high calling demands the ultimate in moral admonition! But what if one of the virtues were inadvertently omitted? Then, as if by Divine inspiration, the writer hit upon the phrase "and all other virtues"! The list is complete. As I say, I don't know whether you ever read the admonition; but if you did, you must have felt truly anointed by the State!

On that September day just before the war, when you gamely faced your first Grade IX class in Huntsville, you were the essence of virtue and grace. Not that you looked virtuous, or even beautiful, by ordinary standards. Far from it, in fact. You were tall and lanky, and your skirt and blouse hung indifferently upon your frame, as if put out to dry. Your face was fair and freckled, and wrinkled like parched fruit.

But when you smiled, your ordinary features took on a certain radiance that was the essence of beauty itself, and we became the willing captives of your charm and warmth. As the year went on, we learned to appreciate that such was the expression that marked you as a great and beloved teacher.

You taught French and Art, surely not the most likely subjects with which to sweep us off our feet in those grim days on the eve of war! Certainly, in that lumbering town of Muskoka, such a cultural diet was not first in order of our interest. By 1939, when war clouds heralded a great adventure for youth, we were more interested in becoming Spitfire pilots than students of French and Art. But you seemed oblivious to those obstacles of the moment and led us through *Le Cours Moyen de Français* with an enthusiasm deserving of a manual of flight instruction!

You were equally impassioned in the field of Art; and even the most unlikely of us looked forward to trying our hand. Oil painting was not on the curriculum. But when you detected that I had a natural talent, you quietly drew me aside and gave me a few old tubes of paint and a brush. Thus equipped, I embarked upon an interest that is with me to this day. Indeed, I am looking at my first painting as I write. It's just a simple rendition of a ship at sea, painted on cardboard. It is cracked across its face, but considers itself lucky to be here, given the tumult of its history. It is my first effort at painting, and I showed it to you right after I painted it, remember? You said that it was very good, so I went home, encouraged. Later that year, I painted a tiny water-colour just about every day for my girlfriend. You know the one.

When I became a teacher, art was very prominent in my classroom. Then I began teaching art at night to senior citizens—and at the end of the sessions they proudly produced eighty pictures for their exhibition! I even painted a few myself, just to stay in touch.

Why just last week, when I attended the funeral of one of my students of the fifties, a former pupil of the period remarked to me that of all the exciting times he had in my class, the most memorable for him were his adventures in art. See what an influence you had?

I gradually parted company with my paints, and did not touch them for fifty years. Then I found myself hospitalized with cancer. During the post-operative period, my daughter Susan suggested that I take up painting again. "It will lift your sprits," she declared, and presented me with the tools, complete with acrylic paints. As if by magic, they rekindled the spirit that you had lit in me more than fifty years earlier.

And it worked. I got into the habit of painting again, and soon became a regular participant in local craft shows. Marilyn, my wife since 1995, carts home jewel boxes, saws, old boards and fungus, all just dying to have their sides covered with the beauty of the landscape, *à la* Miss Fenn. And I thank you for it. When the treasures of my life get into the box to be shown off to people, you can be sure the picture on the wall goes too, and you live again in the showing of it.

Your qualities went far beyond those traditionally assumed in a good teacher. We saw in you a kindred spirit that bridged the gap between authority and rebellion. You seemed to be one of us in our struggle to understand—the companion in the battle rather than the adversary. When you fought to produce the nasal tone demanded of us by oral French, we had the sense that you were struggling with us, and that together we would astonish the world with our skills in a foreign tongue. It was this ethereal skill, this subtle ability to break down the barrier between the known and the unknown that, perhaps more than anything else, marked you as a great teacher.

You were a good friend, too. It was you whom the girls sought out when they had momentous problems of the heart, and you to whom we boys went more furtively on the same subject. It was you who privately helped us in your apartment on the eve of exams, and you it was who dragged many a halting boy to the floor at a school dance. You would ski with the senior classes, cheer us on in hockey and Field Day, and coach us through the mysteries of drama. You knew the vicissitudes of growing up, and more than once you mediated difficulties with other teachers.

You had a certain presence, a kind of glow, that lifted learning beyond mere instruction. You made the most deadly come to life with your humour and zest. You made us productive beyond our nature, because you made us feel that you really cared what would happen to each and every one of us.

As you watched us leave for work or war, you cheered us on, and many of us were thankful for your letters while away. Hugh and I were among those who sought you out after the war. You were ill then, and in retirement. You greeted us like old friends, which indeed we were. The tumultuous years were swept away, and we once again traded stories of our youth, which we had shared with you a world before.

You were gone before I became a teacher. But your mark remained. More times than I can count, your spirit stood beside me, as I struggled to emulate your presence in the classroom; and I suppose that only you and God really know how well I managed. But if it hadn't been for you, and teachers like you, I doubt whether I would have even tried.

Yes, you are gone now, Bessie Fenn. And more great teachers abound now in Ontario than critics will admit. But they, like you, suspect that the Education Act, with all of its admonition, is still incomplete. It misses that indefinable quality of great teachers that has to do with the heart and soul of leading other human beings to reach beyond their grasp, and to enjoy the thrill of it.

You came from Bracebridge, and were truly one of Muskoka's treasures. But your spirit spread its wealth well beyond its borders, and I was one of many who were enriched by it.

Thank you Bessie Fenn.

Lloyd Dennis

Back to the Roots

My world in Ullswater, swept away so suddenly in 1935, remains in my mind still. It's as if every smell, every adventure, each and every bit of experience that filled my daily life were permanently branded upon my mind, lest I let it slip and slide away with time. And to further guard against their disappearance, current events periodically set them on fire to remind me of their presence years ago. A few years ago, I had occasion to drive through the haunts of my childhood, and I used the occasion to seek out the old beech tree that was an object of my youthful attention years ago. It stood across the road from our home, just up from the sandpit where I used to play.

Two things drew our boyhood attention to this tree. One was the nuts which it produced as seeds. Beechnuts, as every country boy knew, were not only seeds; they also offered a clandestine snack on the way home from school. Picking them was a regular habit of ours, and this particular tree was one of our providers.

But the tree provided something else, too. As everyone knows, its smooth grey bark is an open invitation to the artist.

"Make your mark on me!" it seemed to shout in our young ears; and being obedient young servants of nature, my brother and I attacked our tree with our knives, answering that primeval urge to note our passing on the road through life. Our cousin Reg was with us on that first occasion. Before we were through, our initials, a Union Jack and a royal crown were proudly etched on the old tree's bark.

Now, more than sixty years later, it was all I could do to make my way through the underbrush in search of the tree. Oddly, things that stood out so starkly and simply in one's youth seem so different to rediscover in old age. Was it just about here, or was it more to the left? I always remember it standing hard by the sandbank; but no, it must be further back.

At last I stood before it. The tree seemed to have shrunk with the years. Why, I could almost put my arms around it! And ah! There they were, our marks of years ago, L.A.D., V.J.D., R.B., our initials for posterity! And there sat the crown, and the Union Jack, denoting our proud heritage. Mind you, all were a little wizened with the passage of time; but they were still identifiable, should any anthropologist come to decipher them. I stroked them gently, and turned away. After all, I had already made my mark.

More recently, I was invited back to speak to the children at the new Watt School, which now stands on Highway 141 at the corner of the road which leads to the lake, past the site of my old house. I was eager to visit this school, especially since I spoke with the aid of a box of treasures reminiscent of my life at Ullswater. The eyes of the children widened when I pulled the truck from the box, and told them the tale of that long-ago Christmas. And Jumbo's harness, with its tinkling bells, brought my dog back to life for them. One at a time, the relics of my past were pulled from the box to have their moment of glory. Before I sat down, I told the students about the old beech tree, and announced that I had provided a prize to be awarded to any group of students that could find it.

Then a teacher and a group of students approached with a prize for *me.* "Mr. Dennis," said the teacher. "We recently built a trail from the school through the bush to the lake. Along the way, we struck what used to be the garbage dump behind your house. We began to dig, and brought up a number of things that we found there. Would you like to have them?"

Would I like to have them! With trembling hands, I reached out to take a box containing a crumbled old teapot, rusted cans, pieces of pottery—and a stove leg! I gathered the treasures to me and attempted to tell the audience what they meant to me. When I had finished, there was a stillness in the room that was well beyond the ordinary. When I left Watt School that day, I was lighter by far than when I had arrived, leavened as I was by the yeast of an extraordinary experience.

I had been back to the school before, of course. In 1984 good old Watt School had its centennial anniversary, and several of us donned yesterday's costumes for the occasion and enacted the roles of teacher, school inspector, children and parents. It was a great reunion for those of us who shared experiences fifty years earlier.

Even more recently, Ullswater held an anniversary reunion, and I was invited back to take part. The organizers, among whom were my former classmates and their relatives, had done a wonderful job gathering artifacts, and providing a program reminiscent of earlier times. Old acquaintances, unseen for years, suddenly appeared in the new age, like ghosts from the past, and we all became young again as we retraced our steps through former times. When my turn came I drew upon my magic box to tickle their fancy with such items as the Ullswater School bell, the hoop and the honey pail. And I was now able to produce the stove leg as evidence of that sad day when we were evicted. The box of memories was enjoyed by all.

That's not quite true. In later conversation with a local, I was taken aback when he announced that he had the proud duty of moving our empty house to a new location to "somebody who really needed it." He went on, "And another thing. You had no cause to complain. You had no right to stay in that house 'cause you had no deed. All you had was a handshake. If it'd been me, I'd 'ave kicked you out too."

I was somewhat heartened by comments of my friends, who hastened to assure me that this particular local was more noted for his harsh opinions than for courtesy and sensitivity. And I was greatly uplifted when Edith Olsen Smith, in period costume, led the party into a square dance. Good old Edith, Norman, Myron and his sister Madeline, they were all there with a host of others to lead me more gently back to my roots at Ullswater.

Aunt Bessie

The Grimes house stood by the side of the road, dark and silent. Suddenly, the old alarm clock signalled. Louis Grimes swung his feet to the floor and called his slaves. "Bessie, Flossie, Louis, Seth! Get along down here! We've got a whole car waiting to be loaded! Snap to it, I'll get the whip out!"

Louis Grimes was a man of his word, at least with regard to punishment. Those just called were only some of his children who had tasted the lash; and though it was not used on this occasion, they half expected it, and "snapped to it" as they dressed and headed for the tracks, about half a mile away. Mallard's Siding was in the village of Allensville, about fifteen miles north of Bracebridge. It provided a convenient place for the loading of lumber and slabs from the nearby mill. Since the Grimes family lived nearby, it was expected that they would seize any opportunity for work that the siding provided. And since they were expected in school at nine o'clock, the time was ripe for loading.

It was four in the morning. If they hurried, they would have the railway car loaded with slabs in time for a bite of breakfast before heading for school in Allensville. Miss Proudfoot was the teacher. She wrote on the blackboard "Tuesday, October 10, 1904," then rang the bell. Miss Proudfoot was used to children from hard-working families. All were children of pioneers whose families had begun settling Muskoka in the 1800s, and subsisted on bush work or the scant farming that the light soil allowed. The Grimes family survived on a bit of both.

Bessie was born in 1892, and grew to be a tall, rather handsome woman, "four axe-handles across the shoulders," as they used to say. Her rough and tumble upbringing prepared her for whatever fortune had in store, and while still in her teens she had assumed responsibilities well beyond her years. In fact, siblings came to rely upon her when trouble brewed, and she became the undeclared arbitrator when required. More significantly, she became a good cook. It was in this latter capacity that in 1913 she found herself working at Beaumaris, one of Muskoka's flagship hotels on Lake Muskoka.

By this time her personality had attracted a bevy of friends, and a male interest. He was a young Yorkshireman out from England by way of Saskatchewan, and busily polishing his trade as a carpenter by building a dock at Beaumaris. The relationship grew to the point where, in 1914, they put down their respective tools and got married.

Alfred didn't know it but he struck gold when he married Bessie. What she lacked in grace she provided in confidence and determination; and by the time they had been burned out in Milford Bay and had moved to Sudbury, a first son was born. He died in infancy, but Bessie took the loss with her usual stoicism. Her next son arrived in 1918, and she happily bundled him up in 1921 and headed back to Muskoka, where she and Alf worked at a mill in Aspdin. You guessed it! She was the cook. When I arrived in November 1923, the family was complete.

Bessie was busy, but indefatigable. Her circle of friends grew through the Ladies' Aid and the local church, and she could hardly wait for the next square dance. Of course by now, her brothers and sisters had children who found "Aunt Bessie" a compelling influence in their lives. Soon, the appellation became more widespread; she accepted the label from anyone who cared to use it. Then fate closed the mill. Off went Bessie and Alf to nearby Martin's Siding, and while Alf went to prepare a home at Ullswater, she enlarged her circle to include everyone who needed a hand. And picked every berry in sight!

Ullswater was a haven for her, where she sold her precious baking to the tourists, and busied herself in homemaking. Times were tough, but she was impervious to defeat. While Alf worked at the local mill, she kept a big garden, and was lord over the children, turkeys, chickens, two cows and two pigs—with a little help from her sons, of course.

Disaster struck in the middle of the Great Depression. The mill owner's mortgage was foreclosed, and Bessie's family was scattered in the wind. Down but not out, she took her younger son to Utterson to care for an elderly couple, while Alf and the older boy went north in search of work. A year later Bessie was off with the younger boy to cook at Burnbrae Lodge on Peninsula Lake. Three months later, she went to cook at a mill in Falkenburg until Christmas. The winter of 1937 found Bessie and Alf and their older son working in a logging camp in Ravensworth, east of Kearney. The youngster? He was put to board in Huntsville, where he stayed a week—then promptly escaped to join Aunt Bessie at the camp.

When camp broke up in the spring, Aunt Bessie had $30 deducted from her pay for the boy's board. She and Alf rented a tiny house in Huntsville, where she soon got a job washing dishes in a restaurant. (Poor souls. They ignored her ability as a cook, and were the worse for it!) Then it was off to the camp at Bear Lake for the three of them, while the young boarder was put for safe-keeping with a nice old lady named Mrs. Evans.

Throughout these perambulations, she managed not only to keep her family and friends intact, but extended her popularity wherever she went—a competent lass that Muskoka could be proud of, whose spirit was bent, but never broken. Alf was bent, and the boys sometimes cracked under the pressure of circumstances. Not Aunt Bessie!

By now the war was on, Aunt Bessie, Alf and their older son were off to Parry Sound to work in the war plant, while her younger son was put to board in Huntsville.

"I'll miss you son, but you got to have an education. You know how much your dad's countin' on you."

She lived in a tent near Nobel until Alf had built two tiny houses, one for Aunt Bessie and one for his son who was now married. But the "boarder" escaped again, and joined his family in Parry Sound. His mother welcomed him with open arms. He announced that he was going to work at the war plant until old enough to join up and let the Army board him!

As the war neared its end, Aunt Bessie and Alf moved to Toronto to join the workers building Lancaster bombers at Malton. When on leave as a young paratroop officer, her soldier son was given a tour of the plant, and was proud to see his father supervising in the wing section while his mother worked in the foundry. What a fitting place for Aunt Bessie! She furtively slipped her son an aluminum ash tray that she had turned out "in her spare time," as she said.

After the war, she retired to a house in Toronto, which her veteran son bought upon leaving the army.

So much for the *curriculum vitae* of Elizabeth Dennis. And although it hints at the determination of her spirit, it fails to do justice to the courageous struggle that was her companion throughout her life. Like many women of her day, she faced hardship and heartbreak foisted upon her by circumstances beyond her control; and the fact that she faced them relentlessly only added to the assumption that she was equal to whatever came before her. The myth grew, even within her own family, that whatever fate had to offer, "Aunt Bessie could handle it."

It wasn't that easy. Take the occasion of my birth, for example. Already deprived of a home, and over-worked as a cook in a mill while trying to provide some semblance of a home life for her husband and five-year-old son, she suddenly finds herself about to give birth to another! Does she head for the nearest hospital? Of course not! Why she hardly had time to stop peeling potatoes before I popped out—and only added to her anguish by not being a girl! But she soldiered on, and the workers at the dinner table scarcely knew that she had a new mouth to feed.

And we can only imagine the despair that visited her one day in Ullswater, in the home that Dad built. This place had become her world, and it was surrounded by her industry. A bountiful garden of flowers and vegetables framed the roadway, and a network of friends lightened her busy days. To be sure, she was poor—but enriched by a life that can only be bought by care and love. Then it all came crashing down, and she and her small family lost it all. It was the first time that I saw my mother cry. But she well knew that there was "no use crying over spilt milk," as she often said. And even though she suffered the agony of a defeat not of her making, she packed us up and led the way out.

I toss off the Ravensworth saga almost as a romantic adventure. But it was far from that for Mother. Camp cooking was killing, more suited to the strength of a man than that of a woman. But she not only endured it but did the job so well that everyone took it for granted that, whatever the misadventures of the bush, the meals were great! Then I landed upon her. And so great was my dependence upon her that I never gave a thought to the unbearable burden for Mother that I might have brought with me. And the reduction of her wage because of my presence only added to that burden.

She was a champion among champions. I remember the day she left the log drive on the Big East River, came in to Huntsville, and had all of her top teeth removed. She was back on the drive at the end of the day! For me, going to the dentist was a tremendous ordeal. But when I asked Mother about it she only said, "It didn't hurt much because they gave me 'laughing gas'!"

She could have used a lot of laughing gas during the Nobel experience. Not only did she have to endure tent life while her little house was being built, she did shift work at Nobel, five miles away, *and* her son suddenly appeared one day at the tent flap! It was Ravensworth all over again! He got a job at Nobel, fell in love, then announced to his poor mother that he was going to get married—and join the army. Would she cook a wedding dinner?

Aunt Bessie could do anything—so she blessed them both, cooked the dinner, and waved goodbye as he left for the Army a few days later. She then joined his wife in the arduous task of writing to her son almost every day for the next four years. And the letters were punctuated regularly with gifts of chocolates and other delights that she knew he would cherish.

When her veteran son bought that house in Toronto, Bessie and Alf were invited to join him and his wife. There, she quickly became celebrated for her cooking and tea parties, which she held in the garden that her Alf tended so well. She also became keeper of the family soul whenever trials and tribulations arose. She was indeed a famous if unheralded Canadian. She passed away there in 1982, two years after her dear Alf. Both died in their ninetieth year.

And I still have the ash tray!

Englishmen Need Not Apply

History rarely takes the time to record the personal pathos experienced by many of our early settlers in Canada. It is more inclined to dwell upon their "courageous struggle against the wilderness" than to explore the battles fought by individual newcomers as they sought happiness in this new land.

My dad would have been a prime subject for such an exploration. Small and silent, he seemed more fitted for office work than the rough and rowdy life of Muskoka's bush. But that's where he was when I arrived upon the scene, hewing away with the best of them, with the forlorn hope that, however misplaced, he could carve out a living for his small family—aided, of course, by his more stalwart and able wife, Bessie.

He hadn't planned it this way. In fact, he had not figured in the original plan at all. Born Alfred James Dennis, in Leeds, Yorkshire, in 1890, he was the son of James Dennis, who yearned for a piece of his own land. And so it was that greengrocer Dennis forsook his little store in Leeds, with its rabbit carcasses all hanging in a row outside the shop's window, and hustled his family down to Liverpool to sail away in search of free land and fortune in Canada. It was 1901.

James Dennis was not an adventurer; he was merely following the flock of British hopefuls caught up in the frenzy born of the somewhat exaggerated promotion of the fortunes available in the emptiness of Canada. The fact that he was ill-fitted for the contest that awaited him was dwarfed by the very *idea* of owning one's own land, to say nothing of the riches that would doubtless arise from it.

A month after sailing, they landed in St. John, New Brunswick, and went by train to the tent city of Saskatoon. They then struck out by stage for North Battleford. With Alfred and Louise enrolled in the local school, their father took one look at the endless prairie—and promptly got a job driving stage between Battleford and Saskatoon! When he finally got around to filing for land under the Homesteader's Act, Alfred was studying bookkeeping and carpentry, Louise was seeing a young man, and his wife was dying. Fate had changed the whole plan, so simply conceived back home in England.

Young Alfred had followed his father's footsteps, and by 1910 he, too, filed for land. But neither father nor son seemed cut out for farming. Without fulfilling this dream, both headed east, the father to seek his fortune in the United States, the son to search for it in the beauty of Muskoka. Louise was the only one to place her hopes in the prairie—or rather in farmer MacMillan, whom she married and settled down.

Dad found his wealth in surprising fashion. He married my mother. They were, to some, an unlikely couple. She was a sturdy, no nonsense, hard-working girl from a large farm family; he, a slight, rather bookish bespectacled Yorkshireman, who wrote with a fine hand. She was an outgoing rough-cut diamond, big-boned and handsome; he, an introverted, silent though well-spoken skilled tradesman. But Fate had brought them together at Beaumaris, and as I dwell now upon their adventures together, I'm bound to say that both were the better for it.

Dad was a hard worker, armed with skills that went well beyond the bush. But he had several strikes against him. In that era of boom and bust in Canada, there was little room among the "working class" for tender trades or fine handwriting; and for those who spoke with an English accent, the comfort zone was even smaller. Why, some help wanted ads in newspapers even added the warning "Englishmen need not apply." Dad worked, but stayed in his corner.

Of course, Vernon and I were too busy with our own adventures to pay conscious attention to this personal struggle faced by our father. But we certainly were aware that it was Mother who threatened to "take a stick to us"—and often carried out the threat. It was she who seemed to decree the ordinary routines of the family, be it the bringing in of wood and water, or the picking of bugs from the potato plants. It was the result of her labour that produced the delicious odour in the kitchen, not his. And she, rather than he, was the creator of our warm mitts, sweaters and socks. It was little wonder that he seemed more like a wraith than a real person as we struggled for survival in the thirties.

But he earned his worthy place in my treasure chest of memories; and although his presence may have been less visible than that of Mother, it was there, and it had its telling effect. I was said to be more like my dad, while my brother took after Mother. I was more sensitive, leaned more toward books, and "couldn't whip my way out of a paper bag," as my grandmother used to say. Even so, I remember sitting on Dad's lap in the rocking chair while he read to me a story called *The Three Goats Gruff*. Mind you, the fact that I remember it reflects the rarity of the experience; but he did it, and that speaks volumes for him.

The poor man must have suffered painfully during those failing days of the thirties. Unable to roll easily with the punches of the times, or to even find comfort in the good-hearted fellowship of others suffering a similar fate, he struggled silently along, from one demeaning job to another, endlessly looking for that fortunate turn in the road that would allow him to say, "I've made it, Bess! Now you stay home and raise the boys. I'm now the breadwinner of the family!" I can see him yet, leaning into the wind of the darkening day, in his frozen over-sized overalls and old suit jacket, with only a worn fedora to cover his head, heading for home after being told that he had lost his job. During the short time that we had to accept welfare relief, we would go to Raymond with the horse and cutter to spend our paltry allowance. On one occasion, Mother convinced the storekeeper to take back a tin of beans in exchange for a plug of chewing tobacco, for Dad was thus afflicted. I know that he was pleased when she came back to the cutter so endowed. "Here," she said. "Maybe that'll cheer you up!" And I think it did.

I always marvelled at Dad when we went to Church in Ullswater. There, this solemn little man would suddenly become a confident lark during the singing of the hymns, in tune, melodious, and every inch the confident community leader. But, on the way home, he would revert to the quiet essence of failure. Now, as I remember those moments, I can more fully appreciate the value of his moment in the heavenly sun. After all, he *did* sing in St. Columban's Boys' Choir in Leeds and even in Paris before he left for Canada. Perhaps those moments in the far-off little Canadian church returned him, if only for a moment, to his former glory.

There was little comfort for Dad among Mother's siblings. Large and loud, they unabashedly ignored, teased or taunted him until I am certain that, upon occasion, he felt that he had landed in a nest of vipers. One of my uncles was a giant of a man who delighted in picking Dad up and swinging him around like a rag doll, tickling him mercilessly in the process. Another owned a car dealership. Large and mercenary, he took advantage of Dad's weakness for automobiles, and on more than one occasion saddled him with a lemon masquerading as an "excellent deal." Even my grandmother took the odd poke at this "foreigner" who had joined the clan, and was not above chiding him for not providing her daughter Bessie with a better home.

Fortune favoured him in one way. His better-than-average intellect earned him the position of "boss" upon occasion. But even this advantage often had its price. I remember one fateful night in the logging camp at Ravensworth, where he was timekeeper. I walked into the bunkhouse to see Dad being pummelled on the floor by one of the workers. Instinctively, I reached for a sledgehammer that stood against the wall, and was about to save my dad when I was pulled off by two other men, who then broke up the scuffle on the floor. Dad was no match for those ruffians. Neither was his son. After all, I was only thirteen at the time.

It was Dad who blew his nose emotionally when I got the gold medal at the end of public school; and it was he who gave me a little leather belt containing a dollar when I joined the army. And when I returned triumphantly on leave one fine day, resplendent in my brand-new officer's uniform, it was a very proud father who greeted his son with a treasure built by himself. It was a barracks box. I have it to this very day. In fact, it is the inspiration of the theme of this book, for it serves as the "treasure box" which I use to contain the precious links to my past. It opens proudly as I show them off, and the first one out on such occasions is Dad's bible, which says inside, "To Alfred Dennis, on the occasion of his leaving for Canada, presented by St. Columban's Church Choir, 1901."

In 1947, fortune and time finally provided an opportunity for me to know Dad on a different level. I was about to enter Normal School and the world of education, but needed a summer job in the interim. Dad had by now entered Toronto's world of work at the exalted level of superintendent of construction, and was "lording it over" a large crew, bent upon building a new Dominion store. Neither of us spoke of the delicacy of my situation as a son of the boss, but we were both aware of its implication of favouritism. As it turned out, actions spoke more loudly than words. I hired on as a labourer, and took pains to do even more than required. As for his part, Dad leaned upon me a little more sternly than necessary; and as time passed, my fellow workers took pity on me. "Tell the Old Man to back off," they implored. But I never did. Dad and I played our game, successfully and silently.

On his eightieth birthday, I was pleased to honour him by presenting to him a trip to Europe—along with Mother of course! And when I was the recipient of some honour in Toronto, I saw to it that my parents and my brother Vernon were seated front row, centre. In acknowledging my good fortune, I surprised my family by having them stand while I paid tribute to them, whose sacrifice had made it all possible for me. They got a standing ovation; and when my loved ones sat down, I could swear that my dad was taller than before.

The Treasure Chest

They sat in the box, crowded together, with the lid firmly closed. Bible spoke first.

"I'll have you know that I am the most important of the lot of you! Lloyd's father brought me from England. It even says on my fly-leaf, 'To Alfred Dennis from St. Columban's Church Choir on the occasion of his leaving for Canada, 1901.' I was here first, and certainly have the right to lord it over the rest of your colonial chaps."

"Now don't get your precious pages in a flap. When Lloyd was born, I was the first thing in his hands—and stayed there till he was about two years old" It was Rattle, a celluloid relic of Lloyd's birth who proudly comes out of the box every Christmas to adorn the tree. "And furthermore, I still have my rattles, which is more than I can say for some of you guys here."

Doll spoke up. "And I still have spring in my joints! Why every time he shows me off, he shows how I can still bend and twist—and I'm as old as Rattle, for gosh sakes!"

"Hey there! I'm Sugar-Tit. Now I know that this is not a politically correct name, but that's what people called me when Lloyd was a baby. Sure, I'm a simple soul, hand-made by his mother. Take a wooden spoon, wrap a rag around the end, and there I am. Stick me in the sugar and pop me into Lloyd's mouth—why I could keep him quiet for hours. Pretty hard to beat that for a first time job."

Flour Bag spoke from its place around Doll. "I was the true handmaiden of Lloyd's young life. Bessie was poor, but she certainly was innovative! After I was finished with the flour, I was made into so many things it would make your head swim! I've strained syrup, been a tea towel, a table cloth, a dresser top, an apron, a wrapper—why,

I've even served as little Lloyd's diaper—and survived to be fashioned into his underwear—and his dad's too!"

There was a flutter of pages near the top of the box. "I am Eaton's catalogue, and you are all triflers, compared to me. I was Bessie's great companion, Lloyd's first reader, and got to serve the whole family in the end. Why, the whole world knows me for my service to rural households a century ago. No family would be without me, for I offered everything from corsets to horse harnesses. If you get a chance, glance through me. Why, I even have a sheet of wallpaper as one of my pages! And when I was finished as an order book, I retired to the outhouse for the enjoyment of young Lloyd and the comfort of the whole family—one page at a time."

"How come you're still here?" asked Rattle.

"Well, I was forgotten in an old Trunk," answered Catalogue. "Years later I ended up in an antique store and Lloyd bought me."

It was Pail's turn. "Nobody beats me as a handy-man. I first carried honey, but I went on to catch sap, and hold more berries than you can shake a stick at. I had a brother, but he didn't get out much. Spent most of his time under the bed.

"Hear my bells!" It was Dog Harness. "I'm one of the truly great treasures because I am the harness that Jumbo wore when Lloyd was a boy. Every time my bells tinkle, Lloyd goes back to his boyhood."

"I have no bells," said Flat-iron. "But things were certainly humming when Bessie took the clothes off the line."

"And before she put them out," said Wash Tub. "That's where I came in. And both Lloyd and his brother were on intimate terms with me every Saturday night, if you know what I mean."

"I'm Mustard Ointment," said a small white jar holding a bit of red salve. "I may not look like much, but a touch of me rubbed in the right places sure got Lloyd's attention. I, and my sister Mecca Salve, and Raleigh's Ointment, and of course the twins Electric and Castor Oil, were about all the medicines Bessie had for her family. And we did a good job, too. Here meet my cousin, Crown Jar. She was almost as important as I was."

"I only know that everything Pail carried ended up in me," said Crown Jar. "Come Fall, Bessie would have filled about a hundred of us with every thing from syrup, berries, rhubarb and jam to pickled pig's feet. Then she'd store us all in the root house. All through the winter we would feed the Dennis family. We were known as The Preserves, and few could touch us when it came to importance—unless it was Bake Tin, here." Tired out, Bake Tin said nothing.

A small jar spoke up. "Look at me!" she said. "I'm the real thing! I'm full of the original rhubarb preserves that Bessie put in me many years ago. She gave it to Lloyd after he grew up and he still has it. You can see her handwriting on my side. 'Rhubarb,' that's me!"

"I'm Hoop. I and my brother Stick could get Lloyd to school in nothing flat."

"And I'd be in his hip pocket," said Sling-shot. "All the way to school, he would pick up stones, and be lop-sided when he got there."

"And Teacher would whip me out to wave in his face," boasted Strap. "Oh, I was an important influence in Lloyd's life, believe me! He was left-handed, you know; and that was not allowed back then."

"But that never kept him from reading us," said Book. "There are several of us in the box to remind everyone of the important place we had in his life. Why, one of us was even won at the Utterson Fall Fair."

"Speaking of school," said Pencil Box, "You must know how attached I was to the dear boy." A muffled voice in the box muttered. "He hated me. I am Straight Pen, the curse of all 'lefties.' I'm just along for the ride."

"So am I," said Slate. "He gave me up as a bad job, years ago."

"You all know me," said Truck. "I came at Christmas, and I'm still here."

"Remember the Blue Parcel? Well I'm here as a reminder of that great event. No, I'm not the bicycle. But I am the Bill of Sale. It says right here on my face that Lloyd's parents paid $30.50 for one Men's Blue Bicycle, $7.50 cash and the balance in monthly payments. I'm not very big; but I'm an important treasure in this here box."

School Bell, Cow Bell and Coal Oil Can all reminded the others of their right to be in Lloyd's box of treasures; and Picture drew special attention when she explained that she was Lloyd's first oil painting, made when he was fifteen. "Top that!" she challenged.

"I think I can." It was Lloyd's army pack mess tin, issued when he joined the army in 1942. "You are all juniors compared to me. I am one of the treasures of his manhood. And what's more, I contain other treasures of his life as a soldier that are sure to capture the attention of anyone judging our importance in this man's life. There is the 'housewife,' which is really a soldier's bit of yarn, needles and thread; and I hold his identity discs, his pay-book, a small New Testament, his first shaving brush and a stick of his original shaving soap. More importantly, there are copies of letters from his mother and his wife, who wrote him every day. In one letter, his mother advises him to write as much as he can think of in each letter, 'because stamps are four cents now'."

"My name is Sam Browne," said a rolled-up belt, "and I changed his life. He really had to cross the tracks to get me and I was waiting for him when he became an officer in 1943. Of course, I'm too small for him now. He says it's because I shrunk!" His companions in the box chuckled quietly.

"I am Lloyd's parachute," said a billowing bundle on the bottom of this box. "Without me, he would be dead! Top that, if you can."

"I can, because I was his beret when he was a young paratroop officer. I'm not very big, but I sat on the top of the heap, one might say."

"I hesitate to say anything, but you all know that I only joined you recently. I am a memoir written by the father of Lloyd's long-ago girlfriend. He was the one who said that she shouldn't see him anymore, and guess what! I was written many years later, and one of my chapters deals with 'prominent personages' of Huntsville. Lloyd takes up about a page. I guess you can say, 'What goes around, comes around.' Anyway, I'm pleased to be here—even if it is a little late."

"I'm a newcomer, so none of you know me. But I'm pleased to join you at last." It was Stove Leg, resurrected from the dump at Ullswater and presented to the author when he recently spoke at Watt School. But before Stove Leg could go on, Box spoke.

"I get to carry you all around when he speaks about you. And you know what? I am a real treasure box. Lloyd's dad made me and presented me to him when he became a young officer. That was over sixty years ago. Now be quiet, everybody! Here he comes. If he catches us arguing about our importance in his life, he may not take us out to show us off and tell our story."

"That would be a pity," murmured parachute. "I'm dying for some air."

Part of the Grade 10 class photo, Huntsville High School, 1938-9. Lloyd is in the second row from top, wearing the tie. Standing to the right of him are Vern Payne and Hugh Forsythe.

About the author

Born in a logging camp near the hamlet of Aspdin, Muskoka, Lloyd Dennis attended rural Muskoka schools during the 1920s and 1930s. He left Huntsville High School at age 16 to work. During World War II he served as an officer with the Canadian Paratroops.

After the war, Lloyd returned to school, attaining his high school diploma and certification as a teacher (and, subsequently, two degrees from the University of Toronto). He then began his long and adventurous career in education. In 1965 he was invited to join the ministry of education as advisor to the deputy minister. Soon after he was appointed co-chairman, with Mr. Justice Emmett Hall, of the Committee on Aims and Objectives of Education in Ontario. The result was the far-sighted report *Living and Learning*—popularly known as the "Hall-Dennis Report."

Lloyd was the creator and writer of the "Children's Page" which ran for six years in the old *Toronto Telegram*. Books to his credit include, most recently, *The Learning Circus*, about his life as an educator, and *Marching Orders*, his original reminiscences of his childhood and military days. He is also the author of several educational textbooks.

For his service to education, Lloyd has received numerous awards, among them the Order of Ontario and two honorary doctorates from Canadian universities. He is an Officer of the Order of Canada.

Now living in Orillia, he lectures and writes—and, as he says, "celebrate my good fortune to be a Canadian."